HOW TO DO BUSINESS "OFF THE BOOKS"

ADAM CASH

Loompanics Unlimited
Port Townsend, Washington

Published by:
Loompanics Unlimited
PO Box 1197
Port Townsend, WA 98368

ISBN 0-915179-25-3
**Library of Congress
    Card Catalog Number 84-052484**

Contents

1

Introduction

The tax burden on Americans is heavy. The government tells us that it is our patriotic duty to pay our taxes cheerfully. But many patriotic people disagree.

American citizens, whatever shade of political opinion they hold, seem to agree on one thing: their tax dollars are being misspent. Conservatives say money paid for school busing and welfare is wasted. Liberals believe dollars spent on military hardware are boondoggles. Middle-of-the-roaders point to specific government wastages, such as those presented in *A Taxpayer Survey Of The Grace Commission Report*.[1]

Most Americans also see another fact: governments, whether national, state, or local, never have enough money. They always find ways to spend every cent of taxes they collect, and then borrow even more. Americans realize that politicians are not going to lower taxes, regardless of their promises. So more and more Americans are helping themselves lower their taxes.

They don't see much reason to petition the government for redress of their grievances, because it is the government itself which has caused their grievances. So without waiting for government "help," they are taking action, *often illegal action,* to reduce their own taxes.

1

We call these people "Guerrilla Capitalists."[2] We call them that because like guerrillas, they must move fast without extensive support systems, and like capitalists, they are starting and running money-making operations. The government calls them "cheaters," says they aren't paying their "fair share," and threatens to "crack down" on them.

We have found Guerrilla Capitalists to be good honest (more so than most politicians) people working hard at honest occupations, who are only trying to keep a little more money for themselves and their families.

We consider Guerrilla Capitalism to be a very significant phenomenon, because it is a "movement" without leaders, without organization. Guerrilla Capitalists are everyday people who have spontaneously decided to take more control of their own lives, even if it means violating a few tax laws.

Read on, and see for yourself what *you* think of them.

NOTES

1. *A Taxpayer Survey Of The Grace Commission Report,* by William R. Kennedy, Jr. and Robert W. Lee. Green Hill Publishers, 722 Columbus St., Ottawa, IL 61350, 1984.

2. *Guerrilla Capitalism: How to Practice Free Enterprise in an Unfree Economy,* by Adam Cash. Loompanics Unlimited, Port Townsend, WA 98368, 1984.

2

Taxes, Taxes, and More Taxes

Few Americans realize exactly how extensive are the taxes the several levels of government impose on them. Few understand that our governments, federal, state, and local, tax them in ways far beyond those which provoked the American Revolutionary War. Let's look at some specific taxes.

INCOME TAX

This is a big one, the one which costs us the most, and the one that provokes the most complaints. The federal government has the biggest income tax, but most states also tax incomes. Some cities, such as New York City, also impose income taxes. Not only do New York residents have to pay the New York City income tax, but, say, a person living in New Jersey who works in New York must pay the New York City income tax (taxation without representation) and also the New Jersey state income tax, as well as the federal income tax. Some people have to pay three or four levels of income tax — this can be a very heavy load to carry, and small wonder that people look for ways to "cheat."

SALES TAX

Not only are we taxed when we earn money, we are taxed again on the same money when we spend it. Sales taxes are another case where taxation without representation can exist. People who travel and spend money outside of their own home cities or states pay the local sales taxes wherever they are, even though they cannot vote in the local elections because they are not local residents.

EXCISE AND IMPORT TAXES

These are special taxes on certain goods, such as import duties collected by U.S. Customs, and various special taxes on gasoline, jewelry, firearms, and other items. These are not taxes which the retail customer sees, but are paid by the manufacturer, distributor, or retailer and included in the price of the good.

PROPERTY TAXES

Property taxes are usually imposed at the county level, a fourth level of taxation (after federal, state, and city). Usually the money collected from property taxes supports not only the county government, but also the local schools. People without children must pay for the schooling of other peoples' children. Another unfair aspect of this is that parents who choose to send their children to private schools must still pay this tax.

VALUE-ADDED TAX

A value-added tax is merely a sales tax that is levied on the manufacturer or retailer, but does not appear on the ultimate customer's bill. The idea of this is that the taxpayer will not be able to know how much he is paying in this tax. Right now, the value-added tax is widely used in Europe, but does not yet exist in the United States. You can bet our politicians will be trying to get it in, though, and in fact are already bringing it up in Congress, most recently tied to funding for some "environmental cleanup" boondoggle.

HIDDEN TAXES

A businessman usually must buy a license, or more often, several licenses to operate. His customers do not pay these license fees directly, but these costs figure in the businessman's overhead, and are ultimately added to the price of his goods. An apartment house owner must pay property taxes. He adds the cost to the rents he charges, and his tenants ultimately pay. A trucking company pays license fees for its trucks, and fuel taxes as well, and these costs are passed on to the company's clients. So consumers (which in the end is all of us) pay and pay and pay taxes and taxes and more taxes, not only directly, but indirectly as well.

CONCLUSION

With so many taxes eating away at their hard-earned money, it is small wonder that so many people are looking for methods, even illegal methods, to reduce the burden of taxation any way they can.

3

Why Government Spending Will Not Decrease

Nowadays, few can fail to be aware that the government wastes their tax money, but the true extent of this waste is astonishing — and even worse is how waste is actually built into the system! We have read how the Department of Defense has paid hundreds of dollars for such items as screwdrivers and hammers, which are available in any hardware store for a few dollars each, or even cheaper.

Government spending goes up every year, and the deficit grows every year. Let's look at the government debt explosion over the last 40 years.

Harry Truman added $45.4 billion to the debt from 1945 to 1953. Dwight D. Eisenhower added $19.2 billion from 1953 to 1961. John F. Kennedy and Lyndon Johnson added $60.5 billion from 1961 to 1969. Richard M. Nixon and Gerald Ford added $190.1 billion from 1969 to 1977. Jimmy Carter added $182 billion from 1977 to 1981. And Ronald Reagan has added $547 billion from 1981 to 1985.

It clearly doesn't matter which party is in power. Reagan, who has *talked* more about "balancing the budget" than any other President, has run up *triple* the debt that "free spending" Jimmy Carter did! And there is no end in sight.

Put very simply, the candidates on both sides tell the same tired lies year after year, and many voters still believe them.

It is not exclusively an American problem, either, as voters in France, Britain, and other Western countries repeatedly elect the same sort of politicians that we Americans do.

The real problem is deeper than the mediocre quality of our elected officials. Despite strident accusations by some, these are for the most part not evil men, intent on worsening the lot of the people who put them into office. Instead, they are marginally competent men, unable to understand the large issues, lost in the mass of immediate details, and trying to find a compromise between conflicting needs.

Let's look at "defense" spending, to get an insight into why our "national security" threatens to destroy our economy with its voracious appetite for ever more and more expensive weapons.

A common slogan is, "War is good for business." This is true, in the sense that the need for large numbers of weapons and support items do bring large government contracts and create jobs in the areas where the factories producing these weapons are located. However, the basic fact is that our national resources are limited. This is the most powerful industrial nation in the world, but it is still not quite able to produce both guns and butter, despite the assurance of various Presidents that it can. Money spent on weapons has to come from somewhere, and this means one or more of these sources:

■ Taxpayers, who pay higher rates. This absorbs a lot of the overtime pay that defense industry workers enjoy.

■ Diverting from other government projects, such as building and maintaining our highway systems. One result of this is the increasing deterioration of our roads, which will become critical during this decade unless the trend reverses.

■ Printing more money. This causes inflation, as we've seen over the decades.

■ Borrowing. The national debt is out of hand, has been for several decades, and despite the promises of our current President, plans for reducing it are mostly fantasy.

A good example of why our defense spending keeps increasing is the B-1 bomber. The last version of the B-17 "Flying Fortress" heavy bomber produced in WWII cost $276,000 each. Since, bombers have become more "sophisticated," which is governmentalese for complicated, and their prices have gone up to the sky, literally.

When the B-1 was first proposed, over a decade ago, the projected price was about $20 million apiece.[1] This was to be the most sophisticated, versatile, and capable weapons system in our arsenal and, of course, it had its price. The price, in relation to what it could do and the costs of other, already existing systems, did not seem like a very good deal to President Carter, and he cancelled the program in 1977, after the projected price of each aircraft had gone to about $90 million.

President Reagan took another look at it, and decided that the Air Force should have it, but the price in 1981 was at $200 million apiece. By 1983, when the bomber was included in the procurement budget, the price had gone up to $553 million each.

We can't blame inflation or union demands for all these price increases. *The reasons lie in the method of procurement, and the nature of technology itself.*

Each armed service must compete with the other services for a share of the defense dollar. To do so, the service chiefs try to present attractive pictures of their needs, and to understate the costs. For example, when an Air Force General quotes a price for the B-1, he's likely to be giving the price of the airplane alone, not mentioning the cost of new bases and other facilities needed to service the plane, the costs of training the people who will fly and maintain it, the costs of ancillary weapons systems it will carry, and the cost overruns which he anticipates.

With two major powers (the U.S.A. and Russia) competing for military dominance in the world, we find each trying to outdo the other, not so much in quantities of weapons, but in quality of technology. Each power has major research and development programs, constantly improving the capabilities of its weapons. This leads to the dilemma that each administration faces. If they don't buy a weapon today, it will cost much more tommorrow, because of improvements in technology. In the case of the B-1, the changes have been so great that not one B-1 will be operational in its original configuration, and the aircraft delivered to the Air Force will bear the designation "B-1B."

This is bad enough, and the eventual cost of each aircraft could easily exceed one billion dollars, when we count all the expenses that will go with it. However, there's worse.

We occasionally buy "interim models" — weapons that are not really suitable for the job. Sometimes, this is simply due to a mistake. More often, it's deliberate policy, which is hidden from the voters and taxpayers.

Not counting the prospect of bribes to generals and admirals[2] and the expense-paid trips that companies lavish upon them, there is a serious purpose to buying inferior models of weapons. The purpose has to do with research and development, and lead times.

It is impossible to build a modern complicated weapon from scratch. There has to be a design team, and a factory with the proper equipment. *In order to procure the weapon, the Pentagon has to buy it from a company that can make it.* If a company does not get enough government contracts to keep it going, it will go out of business. The skilled workers will find employment elsewhere, and perhaps be lost to the industry as a whole.

Normally, it takes about ten years to design an aircraft and get it into production. This is with an established company that is a going concern. It would take even longer if the project came into the hands of a company that had to assemble a team of engineers, build a manufacturing facility, and start from zero.

This is why it's in the Pentagon's interest to keep the various companies that comprise the "defense industry" alive and well, even if it means buying inferior models. This is not purely an American problem. Other nations face the same dilemma, including the Eastern Bloc countries. They, too, have their unsuccessful models, which they procure while their engineers work on better ones.

Another factor is the increasingly rapid pace of technological advances. The slogan, "If it works, it's obsolete," is not just a joke. It is quite literally true. Better weapons are always on the drawing boards. This means that a weapon that is the latest thing today will be obsolete as soon as the competition brings out a new model. This does not necessarily mean a competing company in this country. To return to the example of the B-1, if the Russians bring out a new fighter with enhanced electronics and missiles that is capable of shooting it down, it's time to go back to the drawing board and improve the B-1, or to design a completely new aircraft.

Often a new plane is not practical because of the huge cost involved. It's cheaper to "upgrade" the existing model, to tack on some improvements that will give it the ability to do a better job. This, too, costs money, and it's impossible to anticipate the cost when ordering the original model.

This close examination of one weapon has given some insight into why the government spends more and more, and why there is no hope for ever keeping spending down.

Also, we must remember that the very structure of our tax system and the agencies which collect the money is redundant and wasteful. To give a simple example, a resident of New York City pays Federal income tax. He also pays New York State income tax. On top of this, he has to file a New York City income tax return. Here we have three redundant bureaucracies doing the same job.

Now let's look at local government and see why *it* spends money wastefully.

We have, by law and by tradition, a system of local governments because of the states' rights provision in the Constitution. We shun a strong central government, even though that's what we have today. Actually, we have the worst of both possible worlds. Let's look at one function of local government to see how this works in practice. Let's look at the police.

Americans don't want a national police force. We like to keep our police forces local, under local control. What we get is a complex system of competing and overlapping jurisdictions, each with its own police force, each following its own laws and procedures.

Typically, a criminal is arrested by a town police force for violating the state's criminal code. He's housed in the town jail until arraigned in the state court, by a county prosecutor. During the trial, he's the responsibility of the county sheriff, who keeps him in the county jail. If he's convicted, and the violation is a major one, he then goes to the state prison to serve his sentence.

Let's take another example, a more common one of a simple traffic accident. Two cars collide in a street the centerline of which is the boundary between the city and the county. A city police officer arriving at the scene determines that, as the cars have come to rest in the county, it's the responsibility of the sheriff's office, and he radios for a deputy to come do the paperwork. He stands by, re-directing traffic, while the deputy is on his way. When the deputy arrives, he pursues the investigation, and cites one of the parties for violating a state traffic law, thereby causing the accident. As a routine part of his investigation, he radios for a "10-29," a routine check to determine if either of the parties is a fugitive from justice. His dispatcher sends a request to the state crime computer, and one to the National Crime Information Center, run by the U.S. Department of Justice in Washington, to see if there are any interstate "wants" on them.

These are normal, routine, bureaucratic complications. They involve a lot of overly-complicated paperwork, which costs money.

Thus, we see that the cost of inefficiencies in our government can't be measured only in money. It's far more serious than that. The net result is that, although we pay more for government than ever before, we are not getting what we're paying for.

Our various levels of government increase in size and cost, but not in effectiveness. In fact, as long as they continue to be organized the way they are, they'll continue to be less effective with each passing year. Less effective and more expensive. That is the hard reality of the "system." That is why government spending will not decrease, regardless of the promises of politicians.

NOTES

1. *The People's Guide to National Defense,* Tobias et al., New York, William Morrow and Company Inc., 1982, p. 346.

2. It's surprising how many military officers find cozy jobs in the defense industry upon retirement. These jobs are partly rewards for past performances in helping the companies that hire them, and partly because they know their way around the Pentagon, as their former service buddies are still in top jobs there. This inside influence is valuable for a company selling to the military.

4

The IRS and
Selective Enforcement

The term "selective enforcement" has become popular in recent years. In theory, every citizen is equal under the law, but anyone even slightly acquainted with law enforcement knows that theory and practice are not the same.

At the most elementary level, the police will make more of an effort to catch a child killer than a prostitute. This is in keeping with the values of the community, and we can't complain about it.

Sometimes, police executives will decide to enforce one category of laws more rigorously than the others, in response to public pressure, or for other reasons. A demand to "clean up" the downtown area of a city, for example, often results in a short-term drive against street hookers and transients. A few months later, when the "heat's off," everything returns to normal. Several years ago, in Scottsdale, Arizona, the Chief of Police announced that his department would no longer enforce the laws against street hookers. Violent crimes had priority, and assigning officers to suppressing prostitution diverted them from investigating more serious and harmful crimes. This is the policy in many cities, although usually without a formal public announcement. Again, we can only agree that it makes sense.

Several decades ago, in New York City, the Police Commissioner announced that his department would no longer enforce the gambling laws. Organized gamblers had corrupted the police officers investigating them, resulting in several major scandals. Stopping the enforcement effort was simply a way of maintaining the integrity of his department. This reasoning holds water.

In these instances, the police executives involved understood the futility of trying to suppress activity that has a lot of public support — the "victimless crimes." Whatever the moral questions involved, efforts to fight prostitution, gambling, pornography, and drinking have failed because a significant number of people continue to patronize the enterprisers who furnish what they want. Without these "dollar votes," all of these fields would dry up very quickly.

Selective enforcement also makes sense in minor offenses, such as traffic violations. In cities where the purpose of traffic laws is to protect the public, not generate revenue, there is selective enforcement. Police officers will ignore minor offenders, such as those who don't come to a full stop at a stop sign, if there's no traffic coming. Instead, they'll concentrate on the dangerous offenders, the reckless drivers and the drunks, who do cause many serious accidents.

On the larger scene however, "selective enforcement" has become a tool to preserve political power. One flagrant example was during the Nixon Administration, when the White House used the FBI, IRS, and CIA to harass those on the "enemies list."[1]

This was the climax of years of imaginative effort by the IRS to get into regular law enforcement. The story of Chicago during the 1920s and 1930s presents a good view of how this came about. Let's look at the official version first:

During the late 1920s the Chicago Police were almost impotent against Al Capone and other mobsters, because the organized bands had very effective methods of protecting themselves. Mobsters corrupted police officers, prosecutors, and even judges to keep out of jail. They had their "bought" legislators who helped pass laws that favored organized crime and resisted measures designed to curb it.

14

Enter the Federal Government. We've seen on TV the remarkable exploits of Elliot Ness and his "Untouchables," who broke up the Chicago mobs with little help from local police. However, Al Capone remained free because he used his organization to insulate himself from prosecution for his crimes. Whenever any gangland murder took place, it was always by a Capone subordinate, and the Big Boss himself was always miles away, establishing an alibi.

At the time, Elmer Irey was Chief of the Intelligence Division of the Internal Revenue Service, and he played a major role in sending Capone to Alcatraz. The key was income tax evasion. Big Al simply had not filed tax returns that accurately declared his income, and this left him open to prosecution under Federal Law. With a long sentence laid upon him, Big Al died in prison in 1940.

That's the legend, and fairly true as far as it goes. Now let's look at the rest of the story:

Chicago was corrupt long before the gangs of the 1920s. The political machine, with its rigged elections and patronage system, had the city in the palm of its hand. When the Italian, Irish, and other immigrants came on the scene and started moving in, the "establishment" saw this as an encroachment on their power. By this time, the original corrupters were literally and truly the establishment, owning the banks and the large corporations. They didn't have to break the law: they made the law.

However, they'd become soft from easy living, and they couldn't prevent the pushy, aggressive newcomers from starting to build their own empires. The law enforcement officials whom they thought were theirs soon changed loyalties, siding with those who made bigger payoffs. Moreover, the new arrivals dealt in the sort of consumer goods and services which have always been popular: alcohol and prostitution.

The establishment had connections in Washington which the immigrants lacked, and were able to seek help from the Federal Government. At the time, the Federal law enforcement agencies were staffed by bright young men who were also ambitious. The young turks of the Treasury Department saw a golden opportunity to hone their skills and earn some good P.R. by playing the role of "gangbusters," whereas before they'd been the "damned revenooers."

Al Capone was the key. Since prosecution of a noted gangster under an obscure statute was a new field, they were able to build up a case before Capone knew what had hit him.

Not to be outdone, J. Edgar Hoover of the almost unknown Federal Bureau of Investigation decided to attain some recognition. He tried to make a name for himself during the "Palmer Red Raids" of 1919, and thereafter beat the drum to warn people about "subversives." During the prosperous 1920s, however, nobody was interested in the "Communist Threat" mainly because it almost didn't exist. The Communist and other radical parties had very few members and practically no power during those years. The FBI languished, unknown and almost inactive.

The gangster era provided an alternate route. There were enough Federal laws on the books to keep the FBI busy, but these were not the sort that attracted headlines. Spectacular shootouts across the American countryside did, however, and this is what J. Edgar Hoover sought.

Carefully choosing his targets, Hoover did not go after organized crime, because it was obvious that if the mobsters could buy off local officials, they might also corrupt FBI agents. Instead, Hoover chose small-time hoodlums, unconnected with organized crime, such as John Dillinger and a few others. By building these people up in the headlines, Hoover gave them formidable stature, and persuaded the voters and taxpayers that his agents were facing a monumental task.

This is the basic story of how Hoover, Irey, and their small staffs managed to turn American history around in midstream. Up to that time, there'd been great mistrust of a too-powerful national government, and especially a national police force. With clever P.R., these Washington bureaucrats were able to persuade people to be more receptive to the idea that national enforcement agencies should have more power and, of course, bigger budgets.

Selective enforcement is still with us. Anyone who's had a run-in with the IRS knows this is true. A tax protester, for example, may not infringe the law, but simply exercise his Constitutional right of free speech. However, the IRS doesn't see it that way. The IRS has the right to investigate anyone, and this power can fall heavily on the subject of its attention. The IRS can, and does, use its investigatory power to punish, without a trial or a chance for defense, anyone whom it wishes.

In certain cases, there's some reason. An example is that of an informer. The "turn in a friend" program is still with the IRS, and anyone can inform on anyone else. The agent to whom he tells his story will, if it seems plausible, fill out a "Form 211" and have the informer sign it, in order to be eligible for a reward.[2] However, not all such "tips" are valid. Some arise out of malice. A spiteful, jealous, or vengeful person can send in an anonymous "tip," and thereby harass his enemy. While at first sight this might seem absurd, the fact is the IRS will investigate if the tip seems plausible. It's merely necessary to sound convincing on the phone to cause trouble with the IRS for an enemy.

"The power to tax is the power to destroy" is such a well-known principle that we needn't discuss it further. What is not as obvious is that *the power to investigate is also the power to destroy.* Let's look at a hypothetical individual, "Smith," to see what can happen to him if the IRS gets on his case:

Smith receives a summons for an audit. This means he must report to the local IRS office with whatever supporting documents and receipts the examiner requests. Smith realizes he'll lose time and pay from work, and phones to find out if he can arrange an appointment during the evening or on a weekend. He finds out that the IRS keeps normal business hours, he must report during those hours,

17

and that how he arranges this, and the consequences to him, are his problem and not theirs.

When he arrives, the examiner questions him about his return, and asks for paper substantiation of his deductions. Smith finds out that this is not like a criminal prosecution in which the defendant is innocent until proven guilty. Instead, the burden of proof is upon him, and he must defend himself against a presumption of guilt.

The examiner decides Smith owes another five hundred dollars. Smith disagrees, and knows enough about his rights to understand that he has the option of an appeal. However, to do this, he has to make an appointment for another session, during business hours of course, and lose another half-day's pay. Five hundred dollars is a large enough amount to make it worth the effort, and he asks for another appointment.

The appeal turns out against him, and the result is that he gets a tax bill for five hundred dollars. The examiner, friendly and sympathetic, tells him afterward that he might have won his appeal if he'd had a tax lawyer or an accountant with him, as a professional would have been better able to present his case.

Smith knows that not being satisfied with the verdict, he has the right to another level of appeal, and that for this he'd better be prepared. He sees an accountant, and finds out that the fee for representation will be one hundred dollars. He'll have to count on losing a full day's pay this time, because the session promises to be lengthy.

Let's leave Smith now to tally the cost to him. Smith earns fifty dollars a day. The accountant's fee is two days' of Smith's pay. He'll have to pay the accountant one hundred dollars, win or lose.

In fact, he's already lost. At least, he's going to have to lose two hundred dollars that he had not foreseen. If he loses the appeal, he'll have lost seven hundred dollars. Win or lose, the IRS will not reimburse him for time lost from work or the cost of his defense.

What can we learn from this? This is not a spectacular case. There was no animosity involved, nor a purposeful persecution for Smith's political beliefs. Smith is not a tax protester, nor a gangster — he's just an ordinary citizen who was the target of a routine examination by the IRS.

Let's now look at "Brown," who is having a more serious run-in with the IRS. Brown's tax return is in dispute. He's done absolutely nothing wrong, and is only guilty of sloppy bookkeeping. He failed to save some receipts to substantiate several large deductions. When Brown comes in, losing half a day's pay, the examiner tells him that he's going to disallow some of his deductions, and that Brown will have to pay another thousand dollars. Brown protests. The examiner is firm, explaining in a reasonable manner that's the way it is, and Brown's going to have to pay. Brown, now angry, tells the examiner that he'll fry in hell before he pays anything he doesn't owe, and stomps out of the office.

The next day at the bank, Brown finds out that his savings account of five hundred dollars has been attached by the IRS, and that he can't withdraw any money from it. On payday, his employer tells him he's not getting a paycheck, because the IRS has garnisheed his pay, and he won't get another cent until the "debt" is paid off. When he gets home, a neighbor tells him a government investigator has been asking about him.

We can stop here. This is enough to show what can happen. We don't have to get into what the IRS can do to a tax protester, or someone's political enemy. The point is that this can happen to anyone.

It's true that people each year are audited simply as part of the bureaucratic machinery, in the Taxpayer Compliance Measurement Program, designed to select a random sample of taxpayers and scrutinize their returns closely to get an idea of how honest people are being with the IRS. This has a side-effect of terrorizing the taxpayers. During such an audit, the taxpayer has to prove every deduction, and every item on the form. This is an ordeal, even for one who has done his homework and is prepared for it.

Perhaps the most disturbing feature of the TCMP is that it falls only upon those who are free of suspicion, because this is a random sampling. Any whose returns seem irregular already get special treatment. The TCMP victims aren't even under suspicion, yet they're penalized. The IRS has no special fund to reimburse the people it calls in for a TCMP audit. They still have to lose time from work. If their returns have been prepared by an accountant, they may have the accountant accompany them, at an extra fee which comes out of their pockets.

The FBI has been accused of many abuses[3] but not of persecuting a set number of innocent people each year to fill a quota. The IRS has the power, and uses it, to punish summarily about fifty thousand TCMP "clients" each year.

Part of the reason is deterrence, or more impolitely, terrorism. Sending a message out to the people that the IRS may, without provocation and without warning, call them in for an audit is a way of telling them the iron fist of repression may descend upon their heads at any time. The IRS feels this "keeps them honest." *Not so.*

We've seen that the underground economy is huge, and so scattered and pervasive that even the government, with all its computers, millions of tons of paperwork, and armies of **agents, cannot get even a close estimate of its size. This suggests that "deterrence" doesn't work.**

Further proof is available almost next door. Anyone who has a close and trusted relationship with a small businessman might, if the businessman really trusts him, get an earful of how he "beat the Feds" on last year's return. The situation is much like that which faced Treasury Agents during Prohibition. There are so many people doing it that the agents can't even find them all, much less arrest and prosecute them.

NOTES

1. *Win your Personal Tax Revolt,* Bill Greene, San Francisco, Harbor Publishing, 1981, p. 12.

2. *Ibid.,* p. 343.

3. *The FBI Nobody Knows,* Fred J. Cook, New York, MacMillan, 1964.

5

How the Fat Cats Avoid Paying Taxes

We've all heard stories of millionaires who pay less in taxes than their chauffeurs. Some might be exaggerations, but they definitely have basis in fact. The "movers and shakers" who run the system have a lot of hidden influence over the law. There are several reasons for this:

■ *They are rich, and part of being rich is to make the best use of the huge amounts of money available.* The expression "the best legislators money can buy" is not a meaningless slogan.

Bribery in the sense of a briefcase full of money is outdated. The modern way to bribe a legislator is through "campaign contributions." This device permits truly huge bribes to be made, above-board and perfectly legally. Anyone who makes such a payment wants something in return. It's naive to think that someone who contributes a huge sum to a candidate's election campaign fund does it because he's practicing good citizenship. He always wants special consideration, although he may not have a specific "favor" in mind at the time.

Another way to bribe a public official is more common in the Western part of this country than in the East. Typically, under the "city manager" system, the mayor is not the actual chief executive, but more in the role of President of the City

Council. He and the other councilmen are usually businessmen, and someone who wants a "favor" can bribe them by "throwing business their way."

We see examples of this when a city council lays out a "downtown redevelopment" plan, often aided by Federal Funding through the Department of HUD. While the selection of the contractors is supposedly rigorously controlled by a system of sealed bids, it's not the same with the laying out of the plan. The corrupt official can make the specifications such that his favorite company is the only one which can bid on it, or at least can bid lower than the others and yet earn a huge profit.

Collusion in the bidding is common, much more common than most people know, even though it is outright illegal. A group of business executives, holding a meeting in a hotel room or at a country club, can decide how to apportion the business among themselves, structuring the bids to ensure that each company makes a handsome profit.

Another avenue of corruption, for a company that hasn't got the whole city government in its pocket, is making an arrangement with a building inspector to permit the use of sub-standard materials and construction methods. This often hinges on "reaching" only one person, who falsifies the paperwork and runs little risk of detection, because he'll probably be retired or dead by the time the use of sub-standard materials shows up several decades from now.

Another way is a stock "tip." The public official, or more often a member of his family, will buy stock following a "tip" from the owner or chief executive of the company issuing the stock, say, just before a 3 for 1 split. This again is an above-board way of bribery which is difficult to prove is illegal. It's a violation of SEC rules, but the difficulty of proof is overwhelming, and we see very few prosecutions for this.

The official who is the subject of this "favor" doesn't face the problem of accounting for a sudden large deposit of cash, and doesn't have to worry about "laundering" it. The bribe comes pre-washed, which makes it not only very convenient, but extremely safe. If he's the least bit prudent, he keeps the transaction above-board, paying the required taxes on it, and thereby avoids any problems with the IRS. The IRS doesn't concern itself with the source of income, as long as the recipient pays taxes on it.

Rich men don't become rich by doing other people favors for nothing. Rather, they manipulate other people and use them, their talents, and their assets for their own benefit. One who makes a campaign contribution, even if he requires no "quid pro quo" at that moment, is making an investment in the future. Once the candidate accepts a contribution, he becomes beholden to his benefactor. He's accepted a favor that will be called in someday. That's how American politics works.

The Internal Revenue Code didn't write itself. It was originally devised by legislators, and has been much modified since its inception. Most of the changes were not to make paying income taxes easier for the average taxpayer, or to make the rules and forms easier to understand, but rather to create loopholes for the wealthy who "own" the legislators who make the laws.

■ *With their wealth, they can hire the best lawyers and accountants to help them avoid taxes.* The rich man doesn't have to forge paperwork to reduce his tax burden. He doesn't need to. He can, upon the advice of his specialists, take advantage of existing loopholes in the law, many of which existed long before he was born, for the benefit of a previous generation of millionaires.

Having high-priced talent available makes a huge difference if there's a disagreement with an agent of the IRS. The working-class taxpayer, if he finds himself required to go for an audit, has to take time off from work, losing pay, and brings his records with him for the scrutiny of an IRS examiner who is a "pro" at extracting taxes from the little guys. Inevitably, the small taxpayer feels anxious and victimized, and with good reason. He doesn't know the ins and outs of the tax laws. If the examiner disallows something, chances are the small taxpayer doesn't know the mechanism by which he may appeal the ruling, or even that he has the right to do so.

By contrast, the millionaire doesn't bother to attend a meeting with the tax examiner, if ever his return comes under scrutiny. Instead, he has an accountant or a tax lawyer in his employ to attend to this nuisance. In this way, he's in a much better position to defend himself than the small taxpayer.

The tax lawyer walks in for the confrontation. Typically, he's got a degree from Harvard or Yale, while the examiner attended Podunk State. It's an unequal contest from the start. The rich man's agent does the intimidating, not the tax examiner. The IRS agent is really on the defensive, as he'll have to substantiate every point he wishes to make, knowing that if there's any doubt, any ambiguity, the tax lawyer is ready and able to appeal his decision, and in fact is paid better.

■ *The wealthy person is free to re-arrange his or her lifestyle to avoid taxes.* The small taxpayer can't do that. He may be free to change jobs, or to move to another city, but not to make a basic break. In any event, his income is so low that he can't save much money even by the most rigorous steps he might take. The millionaire, however, can take advantage of a few provisions in the tax laws, the famous "loopholes."

Income from municipal bonds isn't taxable. Income from stocks is taxable at a lower rate than is earned income. The working-class type who collects a paycheck each week hasn't really got these options. Almost every cent he makes has to go to put food on the table and shoes on his children's feet.

Having a residence outside the United States provides exemption from paying U.S. income taxes. The very rich do this as a matter of course, and indeed own homes in various countries for this purpose. When we read of a millionaire motion picture star making his home in Switzerland, we can be sure that he chooses the place for a more substantial reason than simply enjoying the scenery or the quick access to ski sites. It's a convenient and utterly legal way of avoiding paying taxes on a substantial income.

Another way is to form a foreign corporation in a country that caters to this sort of traffic. Liechtenstein and Monaco are two that are very receptive to sheltering corporations, as their tax laws give the greatest concessions compared to American laws. This is completely legal, and available to the wealthy entrepreneur who seeks a safe haven. Again, the "working stiff" doesn't have this choice open to him.

■ *Taking advantage of the special loopholes that favor businessmen is another way the rich avoid the ravages of the IRS.* There are so many of these loopholes that it would be impossible to close them without scuttling the whole Internal Revenue Code.

The businessman often uses company-owned facilities, materials, and supplies for personal purposes. This is a course open even to the smallest businessman, but the flagrant, high dollar-volume abuses occur in the largest companies:

(1) Most large corporations have company aircraft, supposedly for ferrying their executives to "business conferences" around the country. Typically, there's a company pilot on call and he spends part of his time ferrying around the owner and his family for various personal purposes.

(2) Business meetings. There's no law to forbid a business meeting from being held at a resort such as Las Vegas or Aspen, and it's legal to mix business with pleasure. After the "meeting," which may be perfectly legitimate, the executives take a tour, or go to a nightclub with the company picking up the tab. The time spent attending to "business" during such a junket can be small compared to the number of hours spent seeing the sights.

(3) Entertainment. Even close to home, the company picks up the tab for entertaining clients. The owner or chief

executive often attends these shindigs, and the company pays for the cost of his entertainment, too. Often, an executive will invite a client to dinner at an expensive restaurant, and ask him to bring his wife.

The "hospitality suite" is another way of avoiding paying taxes on entertainment, or declaring it as income. Large corporations maintain such "hospitality suites" year-round at luxury hotels in the area, for the accomodation of visiting businessmen. Often, however, the suite is vacant, which provides a convenient accomodation for the executive and his wife who want to "get away from it all" for a few days, while living at company expense. A hospitality suite also provides a convenient place for an illicit affair outside of marriage.

On a larger scale, some corporations maintain private resorts, often at vacation spots both within and without the country. It's slightly easier to keep a resort going in another country, such as Bermuda or the Cayman Islands, because the IRS has a harder time tracing the exact use the resort gets. The owner or executive can claim that he flew there with his family for a "conference," and the IRS can't subpoena records to determine whether personnel from a client corporation actually attended.

While the small businessman gets away with some fudging, in proportion it's "nickel and dime" compared to the actions of the large corporations. The difference in scale is staggering.

The restaurant owner who appropriates food for his personal use gets away with perhaps a couple thousand dollars' worth a year. One family can eat only so much, and nobody feasts on caviar and champagne every day. Similarly, the gas station owner can only take so much labor and materials for his personally-owned vehicles.

A corporate jet can easily cost several million dollars. The cost of fuel, maintenance, pilots' salaries, hangaring, and other associated expenses can easily amount to several hundred thousand dollars per year.

On a smaller scale, a "hospitality suite" at a luxury hotel can easily cost five hundred dollars a day, and often more. Even with a substantial long-term discount rate, this comes to fifty or one hundred thousand dollars a year. This is for the suite alone, not including additional fees for meals and room service when someone is in residence.

Many lavish dinners pass as "entertainment for clients." The bill for a modest party for four at a medium-priced restaurant is easily one hundred dollars, including drinks and tip. Such executives don't ever take their clients to a fried-chicken or hamburger stand. The cost of a dinner can escalate rapidly, depending on the restaurant and the number of people involved.

We see from this that there's one rule for the little guy, and another for the big boy. It's hard to take seriously any system that not only allows this, but has it written into its laws.

The ones who benefit the most from our government pay the least to support it. The main burden of taxation falls upon the ones who can least afford to pay — which gives the little guy a strong incentive to join the underground economy — to become a "Guerrilla Capitalist."

6

Looking for Loopholes

There's a never-ending search for loopholes, by both small businessmen and large. This is because dealing with the Internal Revenue Service has the characteristics of a game in which the object is to get away with as much as possible without being caught. The people who play this game don't worry much about the "morality" of paying taxes, or the "immorality" of avoiding them. It's a competitive sport. The end: to minimize the tax bite; the means: finding methods of shielding sources of income within the arcane wording of the law. Many high-priced tax lawyers and accountants make cushy careers out of this.

In seeking loopholes, one piece of advice we sometimes see is to be sure to have a "letter of opinion" from a lawyer or accountant.[1] Let's look at this in perspective. Such a letter is a "cover your ass" device only. It does not make a loophole legal. The IRS may still disallow it. The letter merely shows that the taxpayer was following respectable and qualified advice, and not trying to perpetrate a criminal fraud. It's only a device to avoid criminal prosecution, nothing more.

Having such a letter does not exempt the taxpayer from paying back taxes if the IRS disagrees with its contents. It's not a shield against paying interest on any tax owed. It does not even forestall an IRS tax auditor from imposing a penalty payment.

Criminal prosecution is usually unlikely. As long as the claimed loophole is documented, and the taxpayer sets on paper his income and expenditures, the IRS will only go after his money, not his hide. The loophole is merely a point of disagreement, not a peg on which to hang a prosecution.

The single most important fact about tax loopholes is that they're not for the average taxpayer. Most of them are special laws, passed because of machinations behind the scenes by rich and "influential" people who have enough money to buy congressmen.[2] Another point about loopholes is that they're like quicksand, because the Internal Revenue Code changes every year, and what's legal one year is not the next, and vice versa.[3] This makes it very important to keep abreast of new developments.

The most discouraging aspect of most of these tax loopholes is that they apply mainly to people who have large investments. They mainly pertain to investment credits, depreciation rates, stocks, oil royalties, foreign assets, and real estate.[4]

The "new" Reagan Tax Package was really nothing new. It followed in the old pattern of giving tax advantages to businessmen, with the biggest concessions to the biggest wheelers and dealers. This principle, having the big businessmen take all the concessions and sticking the small salaried wage-earner with the bulk of the tax bill, has been the guiding principle of taxation in this country for generations.

While theoretically the law in this country applies equally to all, in practice this is not so. We see this flagrantly in tax laws, because many of the tax relief provisions, although legally applying to every citizen, are simply not accessible to everyone. We don't all own huge tracts of real estate, or oil wells, or have money invested overseas.

Some, however, can be helpful in certain cases. A quick look at them will lay out the high points:

Anyone with money to spare can put it in an "All-Saver" tax-free account, and earn $1000 of tax-free interest. A married couple who want to salt money away can earn twice that amount. This has to be money the person won't need for a long time, and if it's a married couple, they'd better not get divorced. The catch with this is that the individual can't touch the money for a year.

Changes in the laws regarding depreciation rates can be useful for the small businessman. There's a new "Accelerated Cost Recovery System" which enables the taxpayer to take more "front end" depreciation. This is useful for those who buy and sell property fairly quickly, as they can take more than normal depreciation for the time they own the property.

There's an additional loophole if the property is leased to another party. Under certain conditions, it's possible to depreciate it again. This is typical of the fictions of the Internal Revenue Code.

A slight concession to people over 55 comes with the sale of a house. Formerly, the first $100,000 of the sale price was tax-free, but now it's $125,000. A quirk in this law applies it only to married couples, and if they get divorced they each qualify for that $125,000 exemption.

A businessman who needs many deductions for a certain year can choose between depreciating capital expenditures or writing them off in one lump sum. This is called "expensing." There used to be a rule of thumb that only small dollar volume items were allowable as full deductions. The cash value of these depended upon the accountant figuring the tax form, and hovered between $250 and $300. This is another example of a fiction incorporated in the Internal Revenue Code.

A tool costing under that value could be written off entirely the year of purchase, even though its useful life, in common-sense terms, would justify depreciating it over several years. However, to avoid excessive paperwork, this fiction of instant depreciation has long been part of the law.

Now, there are some new guidelines, and the dollar amount may be higher for certain categories. This is a fairly safe ploy to try. It involves a fairly murky aspect of the tax law, and an examiner may not pick it up. "Expensing" a computer, for example, can easily pass. The only risk is having it disallowed, having to depreciate it, and not getting the full deduction for that year.

There's a little-known provision in the IRS code that allows tax-free gifts to employees of up to $400. This need not be in cash, but could be in some other form. This is a useful way to provide bonuses, and deduct them, too.

For certain types of businesses, it's possible to hire minority group members and get a 25% tax credit on their earnings. This rule goes further than ethnic minorities, and includes recent college graduates and others on a list of "target" groups. This is worth a look, and can provide a loophole for the small businessman who can use it.

Incorporation seems very attractive to the small businessman, especially because the tax rates on corporations are currently lower than those applying to wage-earners and unincorporated proprietors. Superficially, this appears to be a fine advantage, but there's a catch. Everything depends on the size of the business. It costs money to incorporate, and this can wipe out any savings. The money involved is not only the initial lawyer's fee and the fee for the state charter, but the extra cost for a more complicated tax return each year. Let's look at some cases:

Tom and Ida decided to incorporate. Tom worked as a free-lance artist, and Ida sold real estate for a local agency. Their combined incomes were not unusually high, and no tax savings were possible, even though they foresaw long-run savings. They paid their fees, filed the papers, and listed themselves as employees of the corporation. They paid themselves small salaries, had the corporation pay for their medical insurance, and put their vehicles in the name of the corporation. The net result was that they lost money the first year. This was not surprising, and they counted on long-term savings.

They soon ran into some problems. To make use of their earnings, they had to collect larger salaries, which were subject to the individual tax rate. They also found that medical insurance was deductible anyway, whether paid by the corporation or individually. The new IRS code stipulates that whatever personal use they made of their corporate vehicles now counted as personal income, and they had to keep logs of their trips and enter their personal mileages. Within their grandiose aspirations, they were "a day late and a dollar short."

"Butch," the owner of a growing business, states flatly that a sole proprietorship is the only way for him. After long discussion with his accountant, he decided that unless his business becomes much larger than it is now, incorporating simply wouldn't pay.

Marriage can be a good loophole. If one spouse has a high income, and the other a low one, filing a joint return in effect averages their income and yields a lower tax bite. A businessman who hires members of his family can distribute the total income among several individuals,[5] which results in lower net taxes for the family.

Individual Retirement Accounts (IRA) for employees and Keogh Plans for the self-employed offer ways to defer taxes that are accessible to some people in the lower-income brackets. The catch is that this requires good money management. Unfortunately, debt seems to be part of the American lifestyle, and not many people can handle this. Anyone who has some money to spare can take advantage of these savings plans with tax-free interest. According to the law, anyone can deposit up to $2,000 per year for an individual, and $2250 for a married couple. The interest earned is tax-free, but there are some catches. There are no withdrawals permitted until age 59½. Anyone wishing to withdraw money from these accounts before then must pay a penalty which more than likely wipes out the earnings. The theory behind the IRA is that the individual gains because his taxes are deferred until retirement, when he'll presumably be in a lower tax bracket.

Practically, this means that "spare cash" must be exactly that, money which the taxpayer doesn't need for current expenses, doesn't need to pay off debts, and doesn't foresee needing as part of an "emergency fund" for the near future. Anyone interested in such a savings plan must calculate very carefully how much cash reserve he should keep on hand in a conventional or money market account to take care of emergencies. A major car repair or medical bill can wipe out a savings account quickly. If there are no ready cash reserves, and it becomes necessary to dip into the IRA account, the taxpayer will be much worse off than if he'd never started.

Another obvious fact is that anyone with a substantial debt should not start any such account. With the high lending interest rates, it's better to pay off the debt, as even the deductions allowed for interest payments are only a fractional saving, and the interest is still an out-of-pocket expense. The tax-free status of an IRA doesn't even begin to make up for this.

There's another catch involved with IRAs and Keogh Plans. The tax rate in years to come may be much higher. While it's true that the present administration has introduced income "indexing," to reduce the inflation creep that put people in higher tax brackets every year, this is something we can't take for granted. We can't predict the future, and those of us who are still far from retirement may find some unpleasant surprises down the road.

NOTES

1. *Bill Greene's 101 New Loopholes,* San Francisco, CA, Harbor Publishing, 1983, p. vii.

2. *Ibid.,* p. 2.

3. *Ibid.,* p. 3.

4. *Ibid.,* pp. 5-33.

5. *Employing Family Members In Your Business: A Tax Bonanza!* by W. Charles Blair and John K. McGill. Taxwise Publications, 1983.

7

Legal or Illegal?

A good question to ask about any tax maneuver you are considering is, *Is it legal or illegal?* If you are going to break the law, you should know what you are doing, and be aware of the possible consequences. Let us examine the possible consequences of breaking the tax laws.

If you get caught breaking the tax laws, there are three possible consequences:

(1) *You will have to pay the taxes you evaded.* The auditor will discover your gimmick and amend your return, presenting you with a bill for the tax you did not pay. This also happens to people who have not deliberately evaded taxes, but who simply made a mistake on their return.

(2) *You will have to pay interest and penalties on the taxes you evaded.* The amount will depend on how much you owe and for how long. We must remember here that the IRS is mainly interested in collecting money, and not in sending people to prison. These penalties and interest are also imposed on those who made genuine mistakes on their returns.

(3) *You may face criminal prosecution.* This is by far the most frightening prospect, at least partly because of the propaganda the IRS puts out about the nasty things it does to tax cheats.

CRIMINAL PROSECUTION

Let's lay it right out again: The main purpose of the IRS is to collect money, not to send people to prison. A prison inmate doesn't earn a salary and pay taxes on it — on the contrary, it costs the government over $15,000 a year to keep someone locked up, and the cost goes up every year. There is also the problem of severe overcrowding in nearly all of the nation's incarceration facilities. If everyone who cheated on his taxes were prosecuted and sent to prison, where would they keep us all, and who could pay for it?

The IRS *will* prosecute a few cases for the intimidation effect, and the mass media will faithfully blare about how tough the IRS is (especially just before April 15!), but the government will not prosecute most cases of tax evasion. The examiner will gloss over the discrepancy and call it a "mistake," or allow the taxpayer to make just about any excuse he wishes. The auditor doesn't want to waste time — he has a quota to meet, and just wants the money.

If the taxpayer gets hostile, or refuses to pay, or starts going on about his Constitutional rights, the examiner will no longer be able to look the other way. Reluctantly, for he will catch hell from his supervisors for not taking care of the matter himself, he will call in a Special Agent and start a prosecution. When this happens, the chances of conviction are actually small, as the government is usually willing to settle out of court, and collect the money.

But as with breaking any law, the possibility of prosecution for tax evasion does still exist. Usually, prosecution is reserved for a very flagrant offender, or a special case. If someone in the administration wants to "get" a certain individual, the IRS will start digging, and then follow up forcefully if it finds any incriminating evidence. Also, those who file "Fifth Amendment" returns or otherwise openly challenge the IRS are likely to be singled out to be made examples of.

Even if the chances of being criminally prosecuted for tax evasion are small, and the chances of being convicted smaller still, there are other consequences that the Guerrilla Capitalist will have to endure. He will have to hire a lawyer, attend court on his own time, lose pay from his job or business, and have both the worry and the inconvenience of fighting a prosecution. By contrast, the IRS Special Agent and the U.S. Attorney don't care about these things, because it is all in a day's work for them. It is what they get paid for, and win or lose, the case will not upset their lives. It will not cause them to lose sleep, or lose pay, or have to pay expensive legal fees.

How to minimize or eliminate the tax bite is a problem we all share, but we are not all equally equipped to fight this battle. Much depends on our station in life.

A contract killer, dope wholesaler, or stickup artist doesn't care about the Internal Revenue Code. Beating the tax laws is one of his lesser problems. Someone risking the electric chair or twenty years in prison isn't going to be impressed by the IRS bureaucrats — a six month sentence for failure to file doesn't raise the hackles.

The very rich, who can invest their fortunes in tax-free bonds and other shelters, also don't care about the IRS. They have the wherewithal to be immune from the IRS, legally.

Big businessmen can employ high-priced attorneys and accountants to help them circumvent the tax laws, taking advantage of every loophole, every ambiguity in the law, and every court decision that might support their positions. They are heavily insulated from IRS harassment.

The small businessman and the wage slave pay the biggest share of taxes, and they are the most vulnerable to harassment and intimidation from the IRS.

But there are ways to work the angles, ways to minimize the tax bite while taking the fewest chances. Choosing a legal or an illegal method depends partly on the circumstances and partly on personal outlook. Some people are more willing to take risks than others.

Let's sketch out the ways to minimize or eliminate taxation:

- Minimize or don't declare income
- Maximize deductions.

That's it. There are no other ways. Every method, legal or illegal, derives from one or both of these.

MINIMIZING OR NOT DECLARING INCOME

Not all methods are available to everyone. First, let's look at the legal methods. Minimizing income in this sense means reducing taxable income. Some forms of income are not taxable, such as municipal bonds, and various tax-sheltered investments. We won't go into these here, because the subject is covered in other books, and because frankly, this book is aimed at the small taxpayer.

One ploy which small businessmen can use, and which is perfectly legal, is to distribute income throughout the family.[1]

Just simply not declaring income will lower your taxes, but can be risky. The two keys to getting away with this are traceability and lifestyle. Briefly, cash and bartered services are not traceable, and one's lifestyle must be consistent with his declared income.

MAXIMIZING DEDUCTIONS

This is what most people do, and some get in trouble, since outright fraud can result in punishment by the IRS. However, there are so many ways of working the angles that the odds are strongly in favor of anyone who goes about it in the right way.

One example of deducting something which might not pass is a fancy boat, on the thin excuse of running an occasional fishing business. The paperwork is all aboveboard, and there is no effort to hide anything or to falsify documents. The worst that can happen is that the IRS will disallow it. The taxpayer would have to pay the tax and be charged interest on it, but the risk is so small that many people feel very comfortable about doing things like this.

The fact of the matter is that the IRS cannot audit more than a small percentage of the tax returns it gets every year, and unless there is something fishy or grossly disproportional within the return itself, the IRS will probably not look twice at it. If they do audit a return with improper deductions, the matter is then one of interpretation. The taxpayer thought he could deduct it, but now the IRS says he can't.

Let us take a look at "Bob," a small businessman who likes to maximize his deductions, and see how he goes about it.

Bob runs a business out of his house, so part of his plan was to buy a bigger house. This immediately gave him high interest payments to deduct, and large parts of his utility bills as well. Bob is an audiophile, and under cover of his business, he has purchased an assortment of very expensive recording equipment. He legitimized this by making and selling self-improvement tape cassettes via mail-order.

Bob needs help in running his business and has solved this problem by putting his family on the payroll. Their pay is taxable to them, of course, but it is still family income that is taxed at a lower rate than if Bob reported it all on his own tax return.

Bob wants to keep his business aboveboard, so he has hired a full-time bookkeeper to maintain his records. Actually, her job takes about two hours a day, and she is Bob's girlfriend. So Bob doesn't have to "keep" his mistress with an apartment and an allowance, European-style. Bob does it the American way by giving her a soft job and generous salary.

Bob has his fingers in a lot of pies, and is always looking for things to "invest" in, and so he writes off a lot of "business" trips. He dabbles in real estate, and deducts an expensive car, which he allegedly uses to impress clients.

Bob is particularly creative when it comes to medical expenses, disdaining the doctors in his own city. Bob prefers to go to a fancy clinic in a West Coast resort town for his annual check-up, which enables him to deduct his entire vacation each year.

We could go on and on some more about how "Bob" does it, but you get the idea. Bob's creative way of arranging his affairs, as it were, enables him to maximize his deductions without too much risk. Bob is constantly studying and reassessing his situation and keeps developing new wrinkles to minimize his tax bite by maximizing his deductions.

CONCLUSION

Different people have different motivations and different goals when it comes to reducing their taxes.

Some people have an urge to "beat the system," and get great personal satisfaction from circumventing the laws. This motivation is quite common, and is not surprising, since we live in a society that is becoming more "managed" and "administered" every year. People become fed up, and want to *do something* to express their individuality.

And of course, there is always the good old profit motive. Paying less in taxes means more for you. This is a good reason to dodge taxes, probably the best and most widespread. As long as it doesn't lapse over into blind greed that can warp judgement, there is nothing wrong with being motivated with wanting to improve one's finances.

All told, the decision of whether to use legal or illegal methods of reducing taxes is up to each individual. *You* must assess the risks and balance them against the potential gain. And finally, you must look inside yourself and answer honestly whether you will be happy carrying out your decision. That's what really counts — whether you like what you are doing.

NOTES

1. *Employing Family Members In Your Business: A Tax Bonanza!*, by W. Charles Blair and John K. McGill. 1983, Taxwise Publications Inc., 201 S. College St. #1300, Charlotte, NC 28244.

8

Will Your C.P.A. Help You?

The answer is *No* in most cases. This may seem surprising, but a look at the CPA's situation will help us understand why. We can start by considering the case of "Ben," an accountant and tax preparer who got into deep trouble with the IRS a few years ago, and spent time in prison on several charges.[1]

Ben had a busy practice, and was the accountant and tax preparer for many individuals and businesses. He was very sympathetic to his clients' needs, and his philosophy was to decide in favor of the client in doubtful instances. He felt the IRS agents could always disallow a deduction if they saw fit, and that it was foolish for a taxpayer to disallow it himself.

His clients were happy with his services, but the IRS wasn't. Ben had given them enough trouble to inspire them to watch any returns prepared by him very carefully, seeking an opportunity to "get" him. This watchfulness paid off. Any tax preparer must use the information that his client provides, and some of Ben's clients falsified information enough to get caught.

The IRS holds the tax preparer equally responsible for the return, and this gave them an opening to prosecute. Ben was sentenced to prison. When he got out on parole, he was so angry at the IRS Agent who set him up that he tried to hire a contract killer to get his revenge. The "contract killer" Ben dealt with turned out to be an undercover agent, and this led to prosecution for attempted murder.

Let's look at each aspect of this dreadful case to understand what happened and why. First, we see that the IRS does not like to lose. Its agents don't like a smart accountant, who knows the rules better that they do, who helps his clients beat the system. They prefer a compliant accountant, who defends his clients' interests, but not too much. The situation is like that of defense attorneys in the Soviet Union. There, as in the U.S., attorneys are "officers of the court," but in the Soviet Union their role is much more limited than it is here. Their purpose is mainly to negotiate a settlement between the accused and the court, to persuade the judges that the defendent was momentarily overcome by capitalist greed, or whatever, but now sees the error of his ways, repents, and asks for mercy. Any Russian attorney who tries to go beyond this and make a serious effort to defend his client American-style, risks being prosecuted himself as a co-conspirator.

IRS REPRISALS

The IRS takes the same view as the Soviet courts. An overly-zealous accountant who gives them several black eyes will go on their revenge list. Thus, they exert very strong pressure on CPA's to "sing along with Mitch." They consider this to be deterrence, and it works. So don't expect too much from your accountant.[2]

Accountants are especially vulnerable to reprisals for several reasons. They're the concentration points for any effort to fight the IRS. An accountant handles many returns. Each taxpayer handles only one — his own. There are many more taxpayers than there are accountants, which makes it much harder for the IRS to give each the same degree of attention.

Most taxpayers "cook" their returns in one way or another. One estimate runs as high as 90%.[3] The IRS undertakes a few prosecutions of these errant taxpayers, and makes sure they get as much publicity as possible. It carefully plays down how tiny this proportion is. Only about 500 convictions occur each year.[4]

Accountants feel the pressure more. If a citizen is prosecuted, most people in the area don't know him. Accountants, as members of a small and tightly-knit occupational group, tend to know each other from meetings of professional associations, and even socially. When an accountant has bad things happen to him, they all hear about it, and the fear hits home.

An accountant who doesn't play along can have some or all of the following happen to him:

(1) The IRS will pay special attention to all returns he prepares.

(2) If their desire to harass him is strong enough, they'll audit everyone who goes to him. If any ask why they're being audited, it's easy for the examiner to slip in a comment that this accountant is known for fudging, and that anyone who employs him can expect an audit. The language will be subtle, the hint obscure, but the message comes across: "You will be audited if this guy prepares your return!"

(3) Auditing each return he prepares will cut into his time, which cuts into his business, as every hour he spends at the IRS office is an hour he can't devote to another client.

(4) The IRS will seek to prosecute him, using a faulty return as a lever.

(5) In an extreme case, the IRS will send in an undercover agent to set him up. Undercover agents are in more widespread use by the IRS than many people realize. An agent will come in, posing as an ordinary taxpayer, and have him prepare a fraudulent return. This lays the way for a prosecution.

UNDERCOVER AGENTS

The agent may be an IRS employee, or a "turned" taxpayer caught with a return that leaves him open to prosecution. In such cases, if the IRS needs a fresh face for an undercover job, the delinquent taxpayer is confronted by an agent who says: "Let's make a deal!" Under IRS instructions, the delinquent goes to the targeted accountant and sets him up for the IRS to catch.

Although instances of IRS agents' tapping telephones, confiscating Social Security checks of old ladies, and other excesses have been documented in Congressional hearings, the activity of undercover agents has not come to light so far, except in the case of prosecutions of mobsters. Among accountants, this danger is well-known, which is one reason why they're reluctant to go too far with a client. They simply don't know if the client is an undercover agent seeking to set them up. Even a long-term client may have gotten into trouble and been "turned."

Law enforcement agencies have a tendency to exceed their authority, and to go far afield on "fishing expeditions." This is why there are Constitutional safeguards against unreasonable search and seizure, and why a warrant is required for an arrest. Otherwise, police officers would be searching and arresting people merely on suspicion, or randomly, just to see what would turn up.

Undercover operations, being secret, are outside the reach of the Constitution. Theoretically, this shouldn't be, but it's very hard to invoke the protection of the Constitution against unseen danger.

We have no way of knowing the precise extent of IRS undercover operations. Are they directed only against targeted accountants? Is there a program to "spot-check" all accountants regularly? We can't answer that confidently. What we can do, however, is make an informed guess at the size of the undercover activity by drawing a parallel between it and the overt actions of the IRS.

The Internal Revenue Service trusts no one, and one of its open activities, the Taxpayer Compliance Measurement Program, is designed to randomly select a number of tax returns for audit each year. These are, purely and simply, spot-checks. From this, we can infer the mentality of IRS agents, and it gives us good reason to suspect that undercover activities encompass more than clear suspects. It's quite reasonable to conclude that the IRS runs a clandestine counterpart to its overt spot-checking program.

This is a heavy burden for the CPA to bear. He knows the IRS is literally looking over his shoulder. This is an inducement to refrain from pursuing his clients' interests too enthusiastically. Yet, some do it. Why?

Some are ideologically motivated, as "Ben" was, feeling big government is trampling the rights of small citizens. Others, by virtue of their positions, have almost immunity to prosecution. These are the full-time employees of large corporations, who can arrange their employers' affairs secure in the knowledge that they're not being set up by walk-in traffic. Others are independent, but service only a few major accounts. The same applies to them. They know their accounts, do not deal with unknown walk-ins, and this gives them a feeling of security.

These high-powered, high-priced accountants are simply unavailable to the small taxpayer. The small businessman or wage-slave who goes to a tax service, or to an accountant with many small clients, can expect only routine processing. Experience shows that they will not go out of their way to suggest tax havens to their clients, even when they're completely legal and above-board.

We see from this that the small taxpayer is on his own, and the best strategy for him to follow is to escape notice. The IRS is much more adept at crushing the small delinquents it manages to catch than it is at enforcing the tax laws on the big-buck boys.

NOTES

1. "Ben" was the author's accountant, until his difficulties with the law landed him in prison. "Ben," of course, is not his real name. This account is partly based on publicly available information, partly on an interview with Ben, partly on reconstruction of what happened.

2. *Win Your Personal Tax Revolt*, Bill Greene, San Francisco, Harbor Publishing, 1981, p. 349.

3. *Ibid.*, p. 350.

4. *Ibid.*, p. 350.

9

Some Underground Economy People

Bill operates an aboveground janitorial service, handling commercial customers. Some of his clients — bachelors, widowers, and divorced men — asked him if he could take on private accounts. Bill decided to do these clients after hours and pocket the income without running it through his books. Bill is running his underground business under the cover of his aboveground business. Expenses for supplies for his private clients are buried in with his commercial accounts, while none of the income gets reported. Bill has been doing this for years now.

Harry, a retired lumber executive, lives in a seacoast town, has a small boat and loves to fish. He goes out each morning and catches more fish than he or his wife can eat. Harry makes extra cash income by selling his fish to local restaurants. When Harry was first making a business out of his fishing hobby, he found that to sell to a seafood store required a license and no store owner would buy from him without it. When he canvassed a few restaurants, he found that a license to sell was required here, also, but he discovered two restaurant owners who were willing to buy from him for cash, since they were tired of being held up by local licensed fishermen. The deals are safe for Harry. The restaurateurs pay him under the table in cash, and ignore his lack of a license because they get a good deal from him. Harry sells only fresh fish, caught that morning. His prices are low, because he has no overhead. Harry has been doing this for three years now, ever since he retired. He has never reported any of this income. Sometimes he barters his fish for a nice meal for him and his wife.

Amanda, a former beautician, still works her old trade underground. Now married and unable to hold a full-time job because of the demands of home and children, she supplements her husband's income by doing her friends' and neighbors' hair in her home. She has her old equipment, which was paid for long ago, so she needed no cash to get her little sideline started. The cash she collects makes a useful, tax-free addition to the family income. She also saves the family money by cutting her husband's and kids' hair. She doesn't report any of her income, which is mostly in cash. Sometimes she barters for babysitting, home-grown garden vegetables, etc. Her friends and neighbors appreciate the low prices Amanda charges, much lower than a licensed establishment could charge.

Joey is a college student who moonlights off the books as a bartender at a local night spot. Joey's dad owned a bar, so Joey knows all the angles of his underground occupation. Joey works the "Happy Hour" five afternoons a week. How he got the job was simple. He scouted likely bars and approached the owners with his proposition: He would work for minimum wage, in cash, with no taxes taken out. Of the four bars he scouted, two offered him jobs, and he accepted one. The owner was glad to get some honest, hard-working part-time help without the taxes and record-keeping requirements of on-the-books employees. And Joey was glad to get a job he could do well, and the hours he wanted to work. Joey is such a good bartender that his tips usually exceed his pay. He does not plan to ever report any of this income. He knows other bartenders who have similar arrangements — in fact, he got the idea from his dad, who often had part-time help off the books.

Lorraine is a widow with a ten-year-old boy, living in a two-story, three-bedroom house. Her husband left her in debt when he died, and she desperately needs to supplement her meager income as a sales clerk. So she rents out her spare bedroom to a college student. Feeling that she simply cannot afford to pay income tax on this extra money, she does not declare it. Her house has a garage, and since Lorraine does not own a car, she rents the garage also. Both her renters pay her in cash, and she leaves this income off her tax return.

Pedro and Juan drive a sanitation truck for the city. From their truck, they run an underground salvage business. It is amazing to them, the valuable items people throw out with their trash. They regularly pick out appliances they can recondition, furniture which needs only minor repairs, and lots and lots of books, records, and clothes, as well as other salvageable items. Twice a day, they stop by one or the other of their garages, depending on where that day's route has taken them, and unload the recyclable stuff they have picked up. The city doesn't expect any of its employees to move very fast, so the small amount of extra time their sideline takes them is easily absorbed in their breaks. On weekends, Pedro and Juan dispose of their repaired "trash" at second hand stores and garage sales. They have never reported any of this income. They know plenty of other city employees doing similar things.

Don trains dogs as a sideline to his regular job. As a dog handler in the Army, he received a solid background in training dogs for obedience and guard work. Don raises guard dogs in his back yard and trains them himself. He can sell a trained guard or attack dog for about three thousand dollars. Don usually has two or three dogs going at once and sells about ten dogs a year. His brother-in-law is a bank officer and helps Don to launder the checks he receives, enabling Don to totally avoid taxes on his profitable sideline.

Janice is a housewife and the mother of two pre-school children. During the day, she runs a profitable business caring for the young children of couples who both work. She currently has ten pre-schoolers in her charge, and the income from this adds a useful sum to her husband's salary. Most of her clients pay cash, and the few checks she gets, she endorses over to the local supermarket, where she is well-known. She advertises mainly by word of mouth, and sometimes with notices on local bulletin boards. Most of her clients are neighbors who know her to be a reliable person who cares about children. They see her not as a businesswoman, but as simply a person trying to earn a few extra dollars by helping out her friends. None of her income has ever appeared on a tax return.

Ralph is an apartment house owner. This is too aboveground an occupation to not report the income, so Ralph has found other ways to avoid paying taxes. Ralph is his own manager and repairman for his small apartment complex, and when he does his taxes, he includes plenty of cash receipts for groceries and liquor and other personal expenses, marking them "Supplies" or "Cleaning Materials" or "Repairs." His favorite shopping place is a department store that sells hardware and building supplies along with groceries and liquor under one roof, and whose cash registers produce unitemized receipts. Ralph manages to "pad" his "deductions" by a comfortable amount each year, saving him considerably on his taxes. He knows other landlords who are doing the same thing.

Red is a welder who cuts hair on the side. He learned barbering in the Air Force. His haircuts are simple, short, and not fancy. They are also cheap. He works at home in the evenings and on the weekends, sometimes in the kitchen, at other times in the back yard. His customers are mostly buddies from work, and neighbors, who don't want to pay the ridiculous prices charged by licensed barber shops. Red will accept nearly anything in payment: cash, boxes of .38 caliber ammunition, home canned food, and even a six-pack of beer, which as often as not, he will share with his client after the haircut is over. Sometimes, the beer drinking starts during the haircut, and a good time is had by all — tax free, of course.

Sam is a retired newspaper publisher. His hobby was calligraphy (fancy hand lettering), and upon retirement, Sam began supplementing his pension and Social Security by doing calligraphy on the side for cash. He gets his business by word-of-mouth, and sometimes puts up cards on bulletin boards in supermarkets, laundromats, etc. Most of his customers pay him in cash, but when Sam gets a check, he simply takes it to the bank it is drawn on and cashes it there — all his customers are local, so this is easy for Sam to do. Sam has never reported any of his calligraphy income.

Lisa is an underground childbirth instructor. There is a trend away from hospital-centered birth in this country because of the expense and other drawbacks involved. Women are becoming increasingly aware that pregnancy is not an illness and are rebelling against the abuses that occur in obstetrics. Obstetricians often induce labor with drugs, to conform to their schedules, not the mother's or the baby's, and use an excessive amount of drugs with sometimes serious effects on the babies, as well as the mothers. Often, they boost their fees by performing unnecessary services, such as fetal monitoring, ultrasonic examinations, episiotomy, and circumcision. After giving birth to her first child, a boy, in a hospital, Lisa decided there had to be a better way. She studied and learned and her next two children, a boy and a girl, were born at home. Both were born with so little difficulty that she decided to teach others about this alternative to the medical establishment. Lisa advertises by word-of-mouth, and with notices on bulletin boards. She uses lectures, videotapes, and printed material in her lessons. She collects in cash, or sometimes in barter. Her husband has a full-time aboveground job, so Lisa does not report her underground income. She has met other childbirth instructors who are doing the same thing.

10

Licenses, Re-Sale Numbers, and Other Business Paperwork

Although we look at these as they apply to particular businesses as we go along, an overview is important. In principle, anyone in business is required to have a business license, following the laws of his locale. In practice, some do and some don't. This is how to break it down:

The businessman with fixed premises (store owner, etc.) or who advertises extensively usually has one, because he's out in the open, and local governments check yellow page listings, newspaper advertisements, and other sources for violators. He can't avoid being seen, and finds it safer to play legitimately.

The undergrounder or part-timer who works out of his home often doesn't. He gets very little exposure, and the effort of tracking him down is very costly in proportion to the amount of revenue recoverable by the government. As the undergrounder tends to operate by word-of-mouth advertising, he runs little risk of detection. He avoids the cost of a business license, and the paperwork trail this creates for the Internal Revenue Service, who regularly cross-checks these for leads on tax evaders.

Another problem is that of a "resale number." This is a license, issued by the state or local government, to enable a businessman who buys supplies for resale to avoid paying the sales tax twice. As he's not the ultimate consumer, he gets the items tax-free, but has to charge his customers tax and remit it to the government. This makes him a tax collector for the government, and also establishes a paperwork trail for other tax collectors to follow.

A closer look at the resale number reveals that it has one advantage and several disadvantages.

The only advantage is that the undergrounder avoids paying sales tax on parts and materials he resells to his customers.

The disadvantages are:

(1) He must fill out forms to apply for the resale number, which means that usually he must present a business license ("d.b.a.") to establish his legitimacy. This starts a dangerous paperwork trail.

(2) When he makes his purchases, he must give his resale license number, which goes into his supplier's records, open to inspection by tax collectors. Anyone without a resale number can buy his supplies anonymously, paying cash, thereby avoiding identification.

(3) The amount of supplies he buys gives tax collectors a clue to his true income, as they keep informed as to markups and can estimate closely the businessman's profit.

The undergrounder must keep a sense of proportion, and understand that by sacrificing the amount of sales tax, he stands to save more on income taxes.

11

Keeping a Low Profile

The Guerrilla Capitalist must work in a somewhat different manner than the visible wage-earner. This is what makes Guerrilla Capitalists different from what people normally call "moonlighting." He comes out into the open to do the work, collects in an untraceable manner, and vanishes once more into the shadows to enjoy his earnings.

The key term is *low profile*. In theory, the government can tax everything it sees. Remaining invisible to the government while earning money is the core of the art of Guerrilla Capitalism. There are many points to watch.

■ Whether you work at your regular skill or at a sideline, collect in cash. Checks are a paper trail to you, and depositing them into your account incriminates you. Throughout this book, we'll touch on this point again and again.

■ Live a low profile. Don't show off your newly-found wealth, and don't appear to live above your means. Don't brag about how smart you are in fooling the government, and don't try any overt protests if in fact you are an undergrounder. Joining a tax revolt movement will only get you closely audited by the IRS. Avoid gimmicks such as the "Fifth Amendment Tax Return," which is illegal and only draws attention to you.[1]

■ In this connection, don't confide in your accountant if you use one to prepare your taxes. Some accountants earn extra money by turning their clients in to the IRS. When we consider that people regularly murder for money, this breach of ethics isn't surprising.

■ While an aboveground business must keep records, the Guerrilla Capitalists avoid records in most instances. Keeping books is creating incriminating evidence. Saving receipts proves the intent to operate a business, which can count against you if you're ever caught.

■ Learn to live a double life. If you work at a "regular" job, adapt to your second one without making it a part of your main one. If, for example, you're a plumber who does a little "outside work," don't have your private customers phoning you at the shop. Have your wife or an answering machine watch the phone for you while you're at work. There are exceptions to this, of course — some employers don't mind, feeling that there's enough business around for everyone. Others allow it if you're moonlighting in a different field and do an occasional free job for them.

■ Business cards can be a problem. While it's incriminating to hand out business cards listing your occupation, one with just your name, address, and phone number is innocuous enough to meet your needs.

NOTES

1. Associated Press, April 20, 1983. The U.S. Supreme Court ruled that citizens cannot claim the protection of the Fifth amendment to withhold tax information from the Internal Revenue Service. In other words, you must fill out the tax form as required.

12

Maintaining Privacy: The Key to the Underground Economy

"You can't fight the system" is a widely-quoted saying. It is mostly true. You can't fight it because most people don't fight it, won't fight it, and in fact will be against you if you try. The key is not to fight it, but to fool it. Beating the system means not outright confrontation, but finessing your way around the rules and regulations.

Fighting the system is what people in the aboveground tax protest movement do when they file "Fifth Amendment" tax returns and other tactics. They generally lose, and even when they do not, they must waste enormous amounts of time and energy in court.

Others suggest different ways of fighting the system and maintaining privacy, such as filling out checks with a non-reproducing-blue pen to prevent their being microfilmed.[1] This isn't really very useful, because if you do it, you are drawing attention to yourself and your activities, and suggesting that you have something to hide.

Another suggestion is to not have a bank account, because the government intimidates bankers into revealing your confidential financial details.[2] But it is very difficult to run a business of any size without some sort of bank account. A checking account is the minimum that will suffice. Many suppliers expect to be paid with a company check, and will question any customer who doesn't have one. A business that requires credit will have to prove credit references and other information that will have to be verified by a bank.

There are other impractical suggestions for maintaining privacy, such as using "dead drops," avoiding the use of the mail, and even writing messages under the stamp on the envelope.[3] These are techniques more suitable to a spy than a Guerrilla Capitalist, and generally involve so much inconvenience that it is cheaper and easier to pay the taxes.

We even see some impossible advice, such as the suggestion that one must never let customs officials stamp his passport, because it makes a record of his travels.[4] The writer making this suggestion does not explain precisely how to prevent a customs or immigration officer from stamping your passport if he wishes.

To maintain privacy in the underground economy, there must be outward compliance with the law, especially in showing a legal means of support.

TACTICS TO PROTECT PRIVACY

What, then, can we do? The answer revolves around tactics, not principles. Some tactics to create financial privacy are using cash as much as possible, avoiding leaving a paperwork trail of your activities, using money orders purchased under false names to make untraceable payments, and keeping some hidden money in travelers' checks, cash, or precious metals.

Each of these tactics has its advantages and disadvantages. For example, paying for everything with cash would work for a very small business, or one that is labor-intensive, that uses man-hours rather than materials, but not for even a medium-sized business. The smart operator will set up a conventional business, complying with the law and use it for a cover for his underground activities, which might include skimming. The moonlighter will hold a cover job, real in both form and substance, to show that he has a legitimate income, and keep his sideline hidden.

Similarly, precious metals are fine for investment or long-term storage, but is impractical to use them for everyday transactions. You can't buy a loaf of bread with a Krugerrand or silver bar.

So we see that maintaining privacy is not a matter of having a hostile, closed-in attitude, but one of outer conformity. Blending in with the crowd is the best way to do it.

It is impractical, if not impossible, to lead a totally underground existence. It is impossible to avoid revealing some personal details to friends, neighbors, and fellow employees. For most of us who have held jobs, there is already much information on file, accessible to the government or private agencies, such as credit bureaus. We can't eliminate this, but we can minimize its impact.

To understand this, we have to get into a little information theory. Those of us concerned with the information about us on file realize that we are not the only ones who have paperwork trails, because the government keeps files on everyone. Files and other intelligence data are a form of information, and this is where the basic principle of privacy lies.

Communications theory tells us that a vital part of distinguishing a meaningful message is the "signal to noise ratio." This means there must be something outstanding about a message in order for the receiver to separate the message from the background static. This seems pretty vague, so let us imagine an example.

Imagine a gun owner and hobbyist who is fearful of gun control efforts. He is worried about joining the National Rifle Association, fearing that if he does, his name will go on a list that will provide government investigators leads if the day for gun confiscation ever comes.

What this guy doesn't realize is that, with almost three million members, the NRA membership list is an unwieldy document, and that investigators would also be working from lists of subscribers to the many gun publications in this country, gun registration records, hunting license applications, and a large number of other lists. He also fails to realize that many people on these lists are not even gun owners, but simply like to read about them. Government confiscation squads would have to plow through each name on the list and conduct an extensive investigation of each person and with current manpower, this would take decades.

This shows us that if we are simply names on a very long list, it is not particularly dangerous for us.

This is where signal-to-noise ratio comes in. A person listed on the NRA membership rolls doesn't stand out from the rest unles he does something else significant, such as getting an arrest record for a violent crime. An NRA member who also files "Fifth Amendment" tax returns, and is a member of a "subversive" organization such as the Posse Comitatus, has been arrested for a violent crime, and has a long record of non-payment of taxes will make waves, and cross-checking, easily done with computers, will "flag" him.

The "flag" is the critical element in attracting the attention of an investigator. This is what makes an individual stand out from the crowds.

Continuing with our discussion of signal-to-noise ratio, many people are concerned that their telephones may be tapped, since there are many outrageous examples of both legal and illegal tapping by government and other agents. In reality, tapping a phone takes both equipment and manpower, and it is impossible to tap every phone in the country. Those likely to have their phones tapped are already subjects of investigations, or have stood out in other ways.

Even if it were possible to tap every phone in the country, someone would have to listen to each conversation, screening it for details of signficance to an investigation. There are rumors of computers which can be programmed to recognize certain words, and proposals to use these to screen every telephone call in the country. With the electronic switching system (ESS), this is actually becoming possible, and one suggested application is to search through the nation's telephone conversations for significant words, such as "bombs," "explosives," or "fuse," in an effort to detect terrorist activities. The computer would "flag" conversations in which these words occurred, for further investigation by a human policeman.

Trying to detect Guerrilla Capitalist activity by using such a computer would be impossible. It would mean "flagging" on the basis of some very commonly used words, such as "cash," etc., and would generate so many "flagged" conversations that there could never be enough investigators to follow up on even a small proportion of them.

We see that any activity that is both legal and ordinary, i.e., one that many other people share, is not particularly dangerous. There is no need to hide the details of everyday life. In fact, any successful effort to hide them will make one stand out from the crowd, which is the opposite of the results sought. Someone without a visible past attracts attention. An employment application, for example, listing no previous work experience and no Social Security number will cause raised eyebrows.

Let us examine two hypothetical individuals to illustrate what works and what doesn't work in keeping privacy and avoiding unwanted attention, and keeping a low profile. Let us assume two individuals, both of whom are gun hobbyists and both of whom are concerned about government firearm confiscation. One is successful in avoiding leaving a trail, and one isn't.

"Mr. A" has purchased several guns, some from licensed dealers, and some from private parties with no paperwork. He plans, if ever there is a confiscation, to give up only the registered guns and hide the "clean" ones. He is a member of the National Rifle Association, and subscribes to half a dozen gun magazines. He has purchased ammunition for each of his guns in retail stores, signing for it each time. The record shows the caliber of the ammunition as well as the quantity. He has ordered reloading equipment from various manufacturers, paying by check and having it shipped to his home. He has been arrested for carrying a concealed weapon, which is only a misdemeanor in his state, was convicted, and paid a $100 fine. He is a member of a couple of extreme political organizations and once was arrested at a demonstration which became violent. He was acquitted for lack of evidence, but the arrest is still in police records. He is also a hunter, has purchased numerous hunting licenses, and once was fined for hunting without a license. His friends, neighbors, fellow employees, and acquaintances know of his guns and his political convictions, since he forcefully lectures anyone who will listen on what he thinks is wrong with the country, and what should be done about it.

"Mr. B," by contrast, is far more discreet. He, too, owns many guns, and is a member of the NRA. He has purchased all his guns from private citizens, paying cash and not leaving his name. He never buys ammunition himself, instead asking a shooting buddy to "pick some up" for him when his buddy is shopping. He owns reloading equipment, all bought over the counter for cash. Since there are no current controls on reloading equipment, he was not required to sign for it or give his name. He casts his own bullets, and obtains other ammo components through the purchases of friends. He doesn't hunt. He is not a member of any extreme political organization, although he is a registered Republican. He doesn't attend political demonstrations and has never been arrested on weapons-related charges. Both at home and at work, he is discreet about his political convictions, preferring to let others do the talking, while he listens quietly. To those who know him, he is a typical middle-class American, a steady worker, family man, and homeowner. Although his neighbors know he owns a couple of guns, nobody suspects that he has fifteen of them and over thirty thousand rounds of ammunition, with some buried in isolated spots.

Which of these guys has the better chance of surviving an investigation? More to the point, which one has the better chance of *avoiding* an investigation?

CONCLUSION

Maintaining privacy involves discretion, not a paranoid attitude. It requires good judgement, not absolute secrecy. It doesn't matter what level of society you occupy, as long as you know how to be discreet and avoid attention. A good example of how not to do it is the case of Howard Hughes. Hughes tried very hard to keep a solid wall of secrecy around himself and his activities, but his extreme behavior only succeeded in getting him several decades of headlines. Many other wealthy people, who knew enough not to be so obvious about their secretiveness, have managed to avoid publicity and attention much better than Mr. Hughes.

You can see from this discussion that keeping your privacy means keeping a discreetly low profile, not building a very visible wall of secrecy around yourself. Blend in, don't stand out, and people just won't notice you.

NOTES

1. *Personal Privacy.* Anonymous and undated, no publisher listed, p. 12.
2. *Ibid.,* pp. 12-15.
3. *Ibid.,* pp. 35-36.
4. *Ibid.,* p. 64.

13

Case History:
Tim, The Underground Printer

Tim runs a small print shop in his garage. His equipment is an A.B. Dick 360, a Multilith 1250, a home-made plate burner, and a home-made padding press. Although he lives in a residential neighborhood, Tim operates his business in his home, because his operation has a couple of features that enable him to get away with it.

First, since he is operating underground, he has never applied for a business license, and thus never gave the city a head start in running him down. He knew full well that often, when dealing with government agencies, people reveal themselves unnecessarily, and give up their right against self-incrimination.

The second reason he remains invisible is that he picks up and delivers the work, and does not have customers parking in front of his house every day. Excessive traffic is one reason there are zoning restrictions, and Tim does not alert his neighbors and give them cause for complaint.

Small printing presses are not noisy, unlike large newspaper web presses, which sound like subway trains. Keeping the garage door closed suppresses enough of the sound so that it doesn't disturb the neighbors, most of whom work and are not home during the day.

He does not have paper company trucks delivering to his door, either. He picks up all of his orders, and brings them home in his van.

Tim operates what is known as a "trade shop," soliciting overflow business from other printers who are happy to have him do work for them at a substantial discount. Without any walk-in trade, he is able to keep his low profile. He is also able to launder the checks his customers give him by passing them on to his suppliers in exchange for paper and ink.

Tim started out as a paper salesman, and therefore knew all the print shops in the large city in which he lived. He knew the mortality rate among small printers was high, and he was able to close in and buy equipment at very low prices when one failed. This gave him an edge over other people starting in the business, who had to pay dealer prices, even for second-hand equipment.

As a salesman, he was able to ferret out the printers who would give him their overflow work, and line them up as accounts. He was also able to procure paper from the company for which he worked, at a substantial discount. This gave him another edge over his competition.

Tim worked seven days a week, five of them for his company and weekends for his underground print shop. As a salesman, his time was his own, and he did not have to put in forty hours a week making the rounds. With a voice pager, he was able to check if there were any calls for him or any problems, and spend many hours at home taking care of his business. Incidentally, he named it "Guerrilla Graphics."

Slowly, the business built up enough to enable him to quit his sales job and work full-time at his printing shop. He'd left on good terms, and was able to continue to buy his paper at a discount, especially as he saved the paper company the cost of delivery.

For several years, Tim ran his operation while keeping his regular job as cover, to explain his means of livelihood to the IRS. When he quit and went full time, he simply stopped filing tax returns, and even went on unemployment for six months. When the unemployment payments stopped, he continued as before, but planned to move out of state before the IRS caught up to him.

He had originally come from California, and still had contacts there. This enabled him to start up again in another location, leaving no forwarding address, and going completely underground.

He accomplished this by renting a garage from a friend, and living in an apartment with his family. With a going business, he was able to rent premises, keeping the payments underground, in cash, so that his friend and collaborator did not declare his rental income on his taxes.

A friend of his was manager of the local branch of the paper company for which he'd worked, and the cozy arrangement which let him buy paper at a discount and launder his checks continued. It also helped for Tim to offer his customers discounts for cash. Later, with a false Social Security number and other supporting ID,[1] he was able to open up a bank account to deposit his checks, and was able to stop offering discounts for cash.

Tim's success story is valuable, not because you necessarily personally can do it, but because it shows a few important lessons in how to start an underground business. Let's see what Tim did right, and what others did wrong.

We've already noted the high failure rate among small print shops in Tim's city. This was for several reasons. Some started by investing money in franchise operations, not knowing anything about the business. The franchise companies are all too happy to take people's money and run them through a one-week crash course in how to operate a small printing press. They're not taking any risks. On the other hand, they're profiting by selling these small investors equipment and supplies at a hefty mark-up. That's how they make their money.

Many who started small print shops invested their life savings in the equipment, and had no operating capital to keep them going during the lean initial period. Not knowing where to find the business, they started cold and scratched for work, while their equipment was standing idle.

Tim, by contrast, knew how to operate the equipment, having worked as a pressman before becoming a paper salesman. He also knew the contacts, which was all-important in his line of work.

Tim kept his finger on the pulse of the printing industry in his locale, and his job enabled him to do this full-time. He knew every print shop owner, knew who their customers were, knew what they charged for their work, and even knew their employees. This was because Tim, like most salesmen, was out for Number One, but kept a friendly, cheerful "front" when he contacted his customers. He also kept his eyes and ears open, and took notes in a small book when he left each customer.

While he never asked his customers what they charged for their work, he often saw their price sheets, and sometimes was able to take a copy with him, on the pretext that he'd pass it on to someone who was interested in having some printing done.

He was able to watch the struggling businesses, and jump in with cash when they were failing and about to liquidate their assets. Thus, he was able to build up his capital equipment while still holding on to his regular job, and at the same time build up a list of potential clients. This was the key to starting a business that required substantial capital.

He eased into his business, first working part-time, and only when the business grew did he go full-time.

He was able to obtain everything at a discount. Not only was he able to get his supplies at cost, but he also bought odd lots from other printers. Printing is very wasteful of paper, and often printers over-buy, then store the excess. There were always odd lots of paper around his accounts' shops, which he was able to pick up for almost nothing. He saved them and offered them to customers who wanted their printing done on fancy grades of paper, at a huge profit to himself.

He kept his overhead very low. Unlike print shop operators who rent commercial property and then have to pay a high rent each month, Tim ran his business at home.

This shows how to do it: Learn the business, have contacts, go slowly and carefully, avoid crippling investments, keep a low profile, have customers lined up before starting, and keep control of every phase of the operation, for maximum profit.

If you're not in the printing trades, forget this line of work. However, be aware that you can adapt Tim's methods to other fields. The principles are the same. Only the details differ.

NOTES

1. There are many excellent books on acquiring bogus Social Security numbers and other "alternate" I.D. Some of them are: *The Paper Trip I* and *The Paper Trip II* from Eden Press, *New I.D. In America,* from Paladin Press, and *Mail Order I.D.,* from Loompanics Unlimited.

14

What Guerrilla Capitalists Can Learn from Spies and Criminals

Because Guerrilla Capitalists violate the law, they are defined by the government as "criminals." This means that because of the need for them to conceal their activities and avoid apprehension and prosecution, it is necessary for them to understand some of the techniques of *real* criminals.

The real clandestine operators, spies and criminals, have developed their tradecraft over centuries, and are more adept at covering their tracks than are people who lead a normal life. In this chapter, we will examine how spies and criminals work, and which of their techniques are adaptable to the Guerrilla Capitalist.

The word "underground" is apt. One of the first uses of the term was the Underground Railroad which was operated before and during the War Between the States by abolitionists, to help escaping slaves from the South reach safety in the North. It had to be kept secret because if they were discovered, the slaves would be returned to their plantations and the operators of the railroad prosecuted.

In World War II, the French "Maquis" were often referred to as the "French Underground" because of the clandestine nature of their activities. This is a good example of a project that was illegal (the occupation forces made the laws, remember) and yet that many citizens felt was not "criminal," because the invaders were unwelcome and did not have the support of the community (despite the large number of collaborators). Among the operations of the French Underground was a system to help the aircrews of shot-down Allied planes escape from the Germans. These networks operated very much like the Underground Railroad in America a century earlier.

Many of the tools and techniques of spies and criminals are not adaptable to the Guerrilla Capitalist. For example, a tax evader should not use weapons. A confrontation and shootout with authorities puts him into the category of the common criminal, and hurts his cause. Normally, the Guerrilla Capitalist's activities are only the concern of the IRS and the real police don't become involved, but an armed confrontation changes that situation in the government's favor.

Similarly, some of the other paraphernalia of espionage and crime aren't very useful to people in the underground economy. The Guerrilla Capitalist doesn't need clandestine radios and suicide pills. The problems which the Guerrilla Capitalist faces in common with the spy or criminal are the ones which interest us, as are the measures which he can adapt to cope with these problems. Let's take them one by one.

COVER

A spy or criminal needs a cover — he must pass as just another undistinguished member of the population. For a spy, the problem is at once simpler and more severe. It is simpler because his agency can easily obtain for him good forged ID documents, and also more severe because if the authorities break his cover, he will face a firing squad, instead of a fine or short prison term as does the tax evader.

The Guerrilla Capitalist lives his real life while working underground, and must keep the two halves separated to some extent. His purpose is to avoid discovery for a very long time and thus his cover is somewhat simpler, but must be more durable.

The spy has to fabricate an entirely new identity in order to inject himself into the other society. His manufactured background may not pass a close inspection. Forging papers is simple compared to "backstopping" a cover. For example, if a spy claims to live in a certain town, his cover will fall apart if an investigation reveals that no one in that town has ever heard of him. By contrast, the Guerrilla Capitalist has an easy task, since he is already a bona fide resident. His cover is his real identity, and a "real job" to provide an explanation of his means of support. Keeping a low profile is the key to the matter.

Some undergrounders need deeper cover, such as illegal immigrants who seek jobs in this country. For them, the problem of obtaining ID is simple, compared to that of the spy in an occupied country. Typically, occupation forces require that every adult carry what has come to be called an "SUI," a Single Universal Identifier. This is usually a card listing the name, address, occupation, physical description and special status, and carrying a photograph and a fingerprint.

There does not exist, and never has existed, any comparable document in this country. What we use for ID is usually a drivers license, a bank card, a draft card, or employee or student ID cards. Some of these are easy to forge or obtain clandestinely.[1]

There is still a good deal of respect for privacy in this country, and this aids the undergrounder, as it does the criminal. It is quite possible to rent an apartment in a city and never meet one's neighbors. Keeping to oneself is not cause for suspicion or alarm. Criminals take advantage of this when they go into a "hideout" (known in espionage circles as a "safe house") until the "heat" is off.

NEED TO KNOW

Both spies and criminals have good reason to keep their knowledge private, and to restrict access to special information only to those who have a "need to know." It is obvious that the more people who know a secret, the greater the chance that the secret will be revealed to the wrong person.

This applies to anything involving security, but most conspicuously to criminals. The police don't publicize it, but most of their investigations center around informants. TV cop shows emphasize physical evidence and the role of the laboratory technician in building a chain of evidence, but in reality, the informant dominates. The lab technician who retrieves a hair sample from a crime scene must have a suspect against whom to match it, and this information more often than not comes from an informant.

Criminals themselves have an interest in not revealing how many of them have been caught because they foolishly bragged about their crimes. You can see from this that it is a good idea to resist the temptation to talk about your financial affairs. Don't tell anyone who has no "need to know" how much you made last year, and in particular tell no one (except maybe for a partner) anything about your underground activities.

Some of your activities will be hard to hide totally. If you moonlight at a second job which is paid "under the table," neighbors will know you are away from home more than regular hours, but they don't need to know how much you earn or get paid. If you moonlight at home, earning extra money from your hobby, there is no need to tell anyone that your activities are anything but a hobby. Bragging can be hazardous to your lifestyle!

Actually, information about what you earn and where you earn it can be quite easy to safeguard. Strangely enough, in America many people are more willing to talk about their sex lives than their financial affairs. This attitude helps to protect you. Always remember that you do not have to reveal anything at all about your finances to anyone who is not an official investigator. Insofar as nosy neighbors and fellow workers are concerned, just tell them, "None of your business." This might seem hard to do, but telling the person who asks an indiscreet question that it's none of his business will be more embarassing to him than to you.

RIGHTS

Spies, when caught, have no rights. Criminals in the USA and most other countries have certain rights. The American criminal is informed of his rights upon arrest by the police officer who reads the "Miranda Card" to him. Basically, the criminal has the right to remain silent and to legal defense. The basic principle, therefore, for both the classic criminal and the Guerrilla Capitalist, is not to reveal information unnecessarily. Many people, both criminals and those with tax problems, do not understand exactly what this means and how to avoid the dangers.

The first rule is: *Don't volunteer information.* If a police officer or tax examiner asks for a piece of information, you may be obliged to give it to him — an example is a drivers license when you are stopped for a traffic violation. Another example is IRS Form 1040, which the IRS requires from taxpayers each year. But beyond this, it is unwise to give anything away unless the authorities specifically ask for it.

The second rule is: *Don't show hostility.* The best way to handle an investigation, tax or criminal, is to play it cool. The investigator has to prove that you are a lawbreaker. You do not have to prove your innocence. Let him do the work. Let him ask the questions, while you answer them as briefly as possible. Remember, you want to play the part of the innocent citizen, willing to cooperate but eager to get it over with and go on your way. Protesting your innocence too much, or showing hostility, will suggest to the investigator that you have something to hide.

Even if you are caught not declaring income, or claiming a false deduction, you should remain cool. Admit only what is on paper, what can be documented, and don't volunteer anything else. Claim it was a mistake. It is up to the examiner to prove fraud — it's not up to you to confess it.

A third rule is: *Don't over-react.* For example, bringing a lawyer or accountant to a tax audit can be unwise in some circumstances. While you *do* have the right to have your accountant, tax advisor, or lawyer present, it can create suspicion if you are claiming to be simply an ordinary Joe with a simple tax return. Corporations always send a lawyer or accountant to a tax audit because their returns are so complicated that they need a specialist. A taxpayer who claims to be merely an employee, with nothing special about his return, cannot claim this, and the presence of an attorney at the first meeting will only attract attention.

An exception is if you have had a tax preparer do your return for you. Then, it is wise to have him present, and the tax examiner will not be suspicious. If you do this, say as little yourself as possible during the meeting. Let your tax man handle it. Resist the temptation to show off your knowledge of the tax laws, because this can work against you if the examiner discovers a violation. If a violation is detected, you can plead ignorance of the law, and this will often pass, because the IRS Code is so complicated that no one person can understand it all.

Let us assume, for example, that you have deducted your mileage driving to and from work, and claim your wages as an employee to be your sole income, keeping your off-the-books activities out of sight. The examiner will explain that the mileage deduction is not allowed as a business expense for an employee, only for the business owner. Then you can say with an embarassed smile, "Gee, I didn't know." He will disallow the deduction, assess you the extra tax, and that is that. But if you have been showing him that you are familiar with the various provisions of the tax code, it will be obvious that you knowingly tried to claim an illegal deduction, and that can mean big trouble.

LAUNDERING MONEY

Fiat currency — good old cold cash — is the basis of the most espionage, crime, and underground transactions.

One of the least told aspects of espionage agencies is their efforts to procure the currencies of the countries upon which they spy. A spy parachuting into Germany or German-occupied territory could hardly expect to get along with a supply of British Pounds or American Dollars. He had to have German Marks, or some of the local occupation currency. Throughout WWII, there was a considerable effort by the Allies to establish dummy companies in neutral countries still trading with Germany in order to obtain supplies of Reichsmarks. Counterfeiting was another way to provide agents with the currency of the enemy, but this was not widespread.

Criminals need to dispose of the fruits of their crimes. There is an elaborate network of fences to buy hard goods at a substantial discount from criminals and to dispose of them in untraceable ways. Fences also launder currency for criminals who steal it.

For example, bank robbers can hardly expect to demand and receive pre-1964 silver coins. They have to take what they can get — currency. Banks impose an extra hazard on them with "FBI Packages" of money with the serial numbers recorded. Similarly, a kidnapper can expect that part or all of the ransom he gets will have recorded serial numbers.

If the criminal is affluent enough, he can flee to foreign shores where he can dispose of the money with relatively little risk or loss. The small criminal must either take his chances that spending the bills will leave a paper trail that points to him, or else get rid of the money through a fence.

Spending the money himself is possible only if he is highly mobile and willing to lead a nomadic existence. If he stays in one place long enough for the bills to be banked and noticed, the authorities would be able to track him down eventually. If he fences the hot money, he must take a loss. The fence will pay only a fraction of face value.

The Guerrilla Capitalist faces a slightly simpler problem. He does not collect marked or recorded money — he only has to make use of his cash without changing his lifestyle so much that he attracts the attention of the IRS. One way is to cache it (more about this below). Taking a vacation under an assumed name is another way, as long as he doesn't use credit cards or checks, which leave paper trails. Re-investing in his underground business is another, as is improving his home. As long as he is not throwing so much money around that people start wondering where he gets it all, he will be OK.

CACHES

Both spies and criminals have needs for caches. They need to hide the tools of their trades, and the products of their activities. The Guerrilla Capitalist can also use a cache, but he has more latitude.

He can use a simple cache, buried underground or concealed somewhere else.[2] Another way to cache money is to rent a safe deposit box under an assumed name, and pay cash for the rental fee. Some undergrounders will open a bank account under their wife's maiden name, although this offers only medium security. Here, a lot depends on whether or not the husband and wife file joint returns, which link their Social Security numbers together in the IRS files.

A son or daughter, if old enough to understand the need, can take out a Social Security Card and use this for establishing a bank account.

DROPS

There are two types of drops: "live" drops; and "dead" drops. The first is a contact with whom the spy or criminal leaves something valuable. A dead drop is simply a temporary hiding place, such as a gap in a stone wall or a hole in a tree, inside which the person leaves something for another to pick up. For example, a spy might leave a canister of microfilm in a dead drop, to be picked up later by a confederate, or a kidnapper might stipulate that the victim's relatives leave the money in a remote place where the kidnapper can pick it up later, after surveying the area for surveillance. The drop, live or dead, is a way to break one's trail.

The Guerrilla Capitalist will not need a dead drop for his purposes. For a live drop, a simple post office box will usually suffice, although a mail forwarding service is safer.

SUMMING UP

What Guerrilla Capitalists have in common with spies and criminals is that all are lawbreakers. The tools and tactics of spies, criminals, and Guerrilla Capitalists are therefore similar in many ways. The methods overlap, and while we despise criminals, we can use some of their tactics. We also dislike spies (at least if they are working for the "other side") but some of their methods are useful for underground economic activities.

NOTES

1. *New I.D. In America,* by Anonymous, Boulder, CO, Paladin Press, 1983. This is a fairly complete dissertation on how to obtain ID suitable for clandestine purposes, and even includes a worthwhile chapter on how investigators trace people. Also see *Methods Of Disguise,* by John Sample, Port Townsend, WA, Loompanics Unlimited, 1984, for information on disguises and other methods of concealing and changing identities.

2. *How To Bury Your Goods,* by Eddie the Wire, Port Townsend, WA, Loompanics Unlimited, 1981. This booklet deals with underground caching. *How To Hide Anything,* by

Michael Connor, Boulder, CO, Paladin Press, 1984. This one covers how to build assorted hiding places, both indoors and outdoors.

15

The Hard-Core Underground Life

Pedro is an illegal immigrant. Although he lacks formal education, his native intelligence is high, and he uses it to earn more money in his adopted country than he did in his native Mexico. His life is almost totally underground, with the help of some friends and relatives.

When he arrived, he "borrowed" his cousin's Social Security card, and used the number to file a spurious W-4 with his employer, the owner of a body shop. Pedro claimed a wife and seven children, when in fact he was unmarried, in order to reduce his withholding to zero. He earned much more money at this than he would have in agriculture as a migrant worker, which is the way many illegal immigrants earn their livings.

He didn't like the idea of agricultural work, because be knew through the grapevine that the employers took advantage of the workers' plight and paid them sub-standard wages. There was also the ever-present danger of a raid by the U.S. Border Patrol and agents of its parent agency, the Immigration and Naturalization Service. He'd even heard that some employers, at the end of the season, would "tip off" the agents themselves, and have the workers rounded up before payday. This was their way of economizing on payroll.

One day, after having worked at the body shop for a year, his employer told him that there was a mix-up with his income tax, and that the Internal Revenue Service had asked for a clarification. Pedro had been well-briefed by his cousin and asked what the problem might be. The employer told him the IRS had no record of him with that Social Security number, and had asked for a correction. Pedro replied that he didn't have his Social Security card with him, but that he'd check when he got home.

The next day, after having consulted with his cousin, he gave the boss a "correct" number, knowing this would keep the bureaucrats going around for a few more months. Before the IRS got back to him, he'd quit and gone to work for another shop, using a totally new identity.

Americans who haven't traveled abroad don't appreciate how truly free and loosely organized life in the United States is. Even the democratic Western European countries have much more official control over the lives of their citizens than the American governments do. To an American, the requirement of registering every change of address with the local police station seems oppressive, but the Swiss live with it. National identity cards, as in France, Germany and other countries, are unknown here. We travel to Canada and Mexico without passports. Even with all the bureaucratic paperwork imposed by the various levels of government here, we are still more "free" than the citizens in most other countries.

Evasion of identity is easy here. There is no law requiring us to be fingerprinted at birth. We have no single document following us around through our lives. A birth certificate is just a piece of paper, without a photograph or any other conclusively identifying data, and access to another's birth certificate is quite easy for anyone who wants to build a false identity.

Perhaps some Americans were surprised to see how easy it is to assume the identity of another person in order to get a false passport, as laid out in the novel, *Day Of The Jackal.*[1]

The events take place in Europe, but the methods are even easier to apply here, where there is less bureaucratic control.

Regarding working in the underground, the case of Pedro shows how easy it is to work at an above-ground job without paying taxes. Very few, if any, employers ever ask to see a Social Security card. Few ask for proof of identity. Some, if the requirements of the job so dictate, may ask to see a drivers or chauffeurs license, or other certificate of skill. Although every job application has space for the applicant to list his education, almost nobody asks to see a diploma. In fact, there have been many instances of people listing false credentials in their application papers, even in such supposedly closely guarded fields as medicine, education, and even the National Security Agency.

Assuming a new identity is easy, under one condition: it must be someone unknown to the person you're trying to fool. This would not apply, for example, to taking over a man's identity to try to fool his wife.[2] Employment situations, though, are different. Typically, many job applicants are strangers to the employer, and claiming a name not one's own doesn't present a major problem. We live in a paper society. Getting a spurious birth certificate or Social Security card is almost routine.[3,4]

There are limitations to the kind of jobs one can get using a false identity. Generally, low-grade jobs are the easiest to get without ID or references. Those which require technical skill usually demand references. This is a critical point, because references are almost impossible to falsify. While it's true that almost anyone can have a fake letterhead printed, and type his own letter of reference, employers who require references will often telephone the alleged former employer. In many instances, an applicant will claim job experience in another company in the same locale, and this means that the two employers know each other. A former employee from the claimed company may be working in the same shop.

Word-of-mouth job referrals are what we call "the hidden job market," and entry into this market is practically impossible for the falsifier. The only workable way for him to get a job is by "walk-in," taking his place in line with many other anonymous applicants.

Another limitation is that jobs which require any sort of security checks are out. Not only the government, but certain private companies require applicants to fill out comprehensive security questionnaires, and sometimes even to submit a set of fingerprints. The questionnaires cover many details of the applicant's life, such as requiring him to list each school attended, and each job he's had. Some require him to list the last five or ten addresses at which he's lived.

Prospective employers in this category defeat the impersonator by running field checks to verify information. An investigator will visit or telephone some or all of the references listed to verify that the applicant actually was there. He may ask other questions pertaining to work habits, personality, and disqualifiers, such as alcoholism, homosexuality, etc. This field check quickly discloses the applicant who has picked up the birth certificate of another who died in childhood.

If you want to earn tax-free income at an above-ground job, the first step is to take a job under a false name and Social Security number. Claim enough dependents to cancel out your withholding. Be prepared for an inquiry from your employer or the IRS when the Social Security number doesn't check out. If you've claimed a number that you simply made up, the computer will disclose that the number either hasn't been assigned yet, or belongs to someone else. This won't happen for many months. This does not automatically result in special agents coming with an arrest warrant. Mistakes in numbers are everyday happenings, and the first step will be to ask for a correction.

This is the first warning. You'll have a few weeks or months before anything serious happens. Use this time to get another identity, another job, and disappear.

Filling in a tax return form when it becomes due is a waste of time. If you have had no withholding, you can't get any refund. In any event, you're not going to be there when the

IRS audits your return, if it does.

The underground life will determine your lifestyle. You'll find it much easier to rent an apartment than to buy a house. You'll need mobility, and moving into and out of a furnished apartment is quicker and easier than getting rid of a house and all the furniture. A large apartment house, futhermore, gives you more privacy than living in a one-family dwelling. Many apartment houses are filled with transients, and there isn't the danger of everybody knowing everyone else's business.

Friends can be a problem. You will probably find the need to make a new set of friends about once a year. If you're very successful in your underground lifestyle, investigators will eventually be looking for you. Although you can easily cover your obvious tracks by moving and leaving no forwarding address, one well-known way of tracing a wanted person is through his friends. If you keep in touch with them, they may unwittingly betray you.

Breaking with your life about once a year requires a total break. Not only does it mean a change of address, and giving up old friends, but also means giving up small details, such as magazine subscriptions and associations. These often link one identity to the next. Sending in a change of address card to a magazine provides an investigator a link, in your handwriting, to your new location. If you're a member of a lodge, or other association, this will link you. A special interest, such as chess, can betray you if you regularly attend meetings of a chess club and participate in tournaments.

Finally, we have to look at your emotional stamina. Is the underground life, with its rootlessness, really for you? Americans are mobile people, moving from one end of the country to the other more than any people in history, but usually they keep in contact with their friends and relatives, and seek to settle down when they arrive. The underground life is truly a nomadic existence, and although it seems attractive at first, it can become tiring as the years go by. It requires a total commitment to the demands of the lifestyle, and constant attention to details to avoid exposure.

In one sense, it's very much like being an enemy agent in your own country. It means living a "cover," always watchful, and simply doesn't permit the activities that many people enjoy, such as settling down, getting married, and raising a family. Not everyone can handle this.

You're the only one who can tell if this lifestyle is for you. Ask yourself if you want to live under the conditions laid out here. If your situation is like Pedro, you might find it easy to adapt. You might find the prospect unattractive, and might prefer to live an above-ground life, with only a part of your activities hidden from the light of day.

NOTES

1. *The Day of the Jackal,* Frederick Forsyth, New York, The Viking Press, 1971, pp. 71-104. In these pages, Forsyth uses his fictional character to demonstrate how easy it is to procure several different identities by different methods. One is by assuming the identity of a person his own age who died as a child, getting a copy of the birth certificate and using that to obtain a passport. Another is by stealing the passports of men who resemble him closely enough to permit his disguising himself as them. A third method is to forge the documents outright. Not only is "Jackal" an exciting novel, it is realistic.

2. *Methods Of Disguise,* John Sample, Port Townsend, WA, Loompanics Unlimited, 1984. As explained in this book, trying to fool close friends and associates is almost impossible. Disguise has its limitations, even with extreme methods such as plastic surgery. Assuming the identity of a person whom your contacts have never met, on the other hand, is ridiculously easy.

3. *The Paper Trip, Volumes I and II,* Barry Reid, Fountain Valley, CA, Eden Press. These two books give detailed instructions on getting fake ID, not only detailing the methods step by step, but even providing the address of the

public records office for every state, and artwork for forgeries. With these volumes, it's possible to put together almost any sort of ID needed.

4. *New ID in America,* Anonymous, Boulder, CO, Paladin Press, 1983. This book not only gives information on how to procure new and serious ID, but much background material on how to use it, and what pitfalls to avoid. Anyone contemplating getting false ID should read this to get a well-rounded picture of what he faces.

16

A Quick Look at the IRS

It's popular in some circles to refer to the Internal Revenue Service as "The American Gestapo." This is a bad comparison. The IRS simply is not as efficient and capable as the Gestapo was. Making such a comparison exaggerates the proficiency of the IRS, and makes it seem a much more formidable opponent than it is in real life. To show the difference, let's first take a quick look at the Gestapo, as it really was.

The *Geheime Staats-Polizei,* the Gestapo, was an agency for internal security and counter-espionage. Contrary to the image presented in films and television programs, it was not composed of jack-booted sadists recruited from prisons and mental hospitals. The Gestapo officers were experienced criminal investigators, recruited from the best of the country's police forces. Mueller, the Chief of the Gestapo, came from the Karlsruhe Criminal Investigation Department. Others were recruited from the brightest university graduates, with many having advanced degrees.

The Gestapo got a bad image because of the activities of people such as Adolph Eichmann, who was involved in the Jewish persecutions. Actually, this was one small part of the Gestapo's efforts, and the sub-section assigned this duty was staffed by lackluster people such as Eichmann. The much-publicized Eichmann trial showed the sort of person he was: a clerk, who scheduled deportations for the Gestapo. Despite his rank of Colonel, he was simply a clerk in his function, a colorless figure who performed a routine job. The picture he presented on television was unimpressive: an unimaginative person doing a dull job.

In fact, it was. The Jewish persecutions did not require the talents of the cream of the crop. Rounding up and deporting civilians, including women and children, was not a demanding task, compared to running down skilled enemy agents, and the Gestapo did not assign their best people to it.

The intrepid and imaginative investigators handled the hard jobs: intercepting agents' radio transmissions, code-breaking, tracing networks of spies, arresting and "turning" them, and deception operations. Contrary to Allied propaganda, the Gestapo did not arrest agents and immediately beat them up to force confessions. It wasn't in their best interest to do so.

Instead, they first tried a soft approach, persuading the arrestees that they had more to gain by cooperation than by resistance. This is exactly the technique used by criminal investigators throughout the world. An arrestee who cooperates, who talks and turns in other members of his organization, is much more useful to a police force, including the Gestapo, than one who keeps silent and goes to his execution without talking.

The Gestapo, like other security forces, turned many arrestees into double agents, pretending to be still working for the Allies while really obeying Gestapo orders. One of the most-ignored stories of World War II is how successfully the Gestapo did this. Producing propaganda about sadistic tortures attracts more readers than telling a true story about the patient and diligent efforts that produce more rewarding results in the end. It's also self-serving to portray an enemy as ruthless and sadistic instead of admitting that he's very clever and capable.

The Gestapo was so feared, not because it was composed of criminal sadists, but because it was so effective. At the time, it was one of the very best security police forces in the world, and even today there are not many security organizations that equal it.

Now let's turn to the IRS, and see it as it *really* is. Despite its sophisticated computers, it still depends on human material for its tasks. Instead of daring and intrepid investigators, we see bureaucrats in three-piece suits, more concerned with fringe benefits and retirement than with doing their jobs well. There has been falsification of their skills. We remember the TV series *The Untouchables,* with Elliot Ness as the courageous hero who took on the mob. Actually, although the real-life Ness was a Treasury Agent, he did not handle all the cases presented on TV, and most of his work was not as exciting as the series portrayed.

Physically, an office of the IRS looks very much like the Social Security Administration, the State Corporation Commission, or the Office of Management and Budget. We see the same desks, the same clocks on the wall (avidly watched by the paper-pushers), and the same file cabinets.

We see basically the same people. Only the names are different. The term "paper pusher" is accurate and descriptive, because these peoples' work is ruled by endless reports, forms, regulations, procedural guidelines, and schedules. Their method of working depends on the framework laid out in their operations manual.

The main motivation of these people is a package of salary, perquisites and fringe benefits that goes with the job. Many of them spend more time worrying about their fringe benefits than in doing their jobs. Another serious concern is abiding by the multitude of regulations that rules their lives and not falling into a trap in which they'll be liable for blame, thereby endangering their chances for promotion, their retirement benefits, and even their careers.

This leads to the "CYA" (cover your ass) mentality. An employee will strive to avoid taking any risks, even in pursuit of the agency's objectives, because taking risks, especially if they're outside the guidelines and rules that govern him, are dangerous to his occupational health. There is no spirit of bold entrepreneurship in the IRS, only a dull and plodding adherence to procedures.

Much of what we hear and read about the IRS is propaganda, news slanted to give a false impression and exaggerate the IRS's effectiveness. We read about massive central computers recording every detail of everyone's finances and armies of agents and examiners poring over tax returns and masses of other forms to put together their picture of tax evaders.

Occasionally, we read of IRS participation in the various "Organized Crime Strike Forces" that crop up in various parts of the country. These titles give an impression of massive effectiveness, but the reality is quite different. A "strike force" peopled by agents in three-piece suits is laughable. It is mostly ineffective, because its method of operation is chasing paperwork instead of chasing lawbreakers. Although we read that Elliot Ness and his crew put away Al Capone,[1] his mob and its descendants live on.

Organized crime today is stronger than ever, despite the many millions of man-hours of enforcement effort, and the mass of publicity. Arresting and convicting a few men with Italian surnames does not put the Mob out of business.

If the IRS can't "get" the big operators, then what *can* it do? It can catch the inexperienced and unwary, who don't know how to take simple precautions to protect themselves. The small evaders, just starting out, and the naive ones, are its victims.

It's true the IRS has computers, but anyone who has had a foul-up on his computer-generated utility bill has an idea of the limitations of computers. Anyone who has a legitimate tax refund coming understands that the IRS computers don't cope well with even routine work.

Computers are wonderful machines, but they can only do what their masters tell them to do. Dull and unimaginative people will operate their computers in dull and unimaginative ways.

This is why a person can take an above-ground job, giving a false Social Security number and falsifying his W-4 to have nothing withheld, and the IRS won't catch up to him for months or years. All this information goes into a computer, which operates with the speed of light, yet what do the human operators do with it? Drowning in paperwork, they move at a snail's pace.

If the undergrounder understands the IRS and how it operates, understands its few strengths and great limitations, and makes good use of this information, he'll be able to tailor his effort to his needs and avoid the mistakes that trap the unwary. With proper information, and proper use of that information, he'll be able to earn money and keep what he earns.

NOTES

1. If you have read various books dealing with the events surrounding the prosecution of Al Capone, you'll find the authors disagree. Various people have scrambled to get credit for the effort against Al Capone, and it's hard to get a clear idea of exactly who did what. The only clear facts that emerge from the whole dismal story is that Al Capone was so powerful, and so effective, that he could operate out in the open, suborning police officials and running his business unimpeded by all except other Mob leaders who operated the way he did. What stopped smuggling and bootlegging was repeal of Prohibition, not hordes of enforcement agents, and countless man-hours and dollars went to putting Capone away for just a few years, after a long career. Capone finally died of syphilis, not electrocution.

17

Big Brother — How Vulnerable are You?

As a Guerrilla Capitalist, you may be vulnerable to two things: tax collection and prosecution. You must be aware that the government is very serious about collecting taxes, and often takes extreme steps to collect.

Collecting and prosecution are complex, but compared with the steps the government takes to discover tax evaders, very simple. The overriding fact is that the person who gets a tax bill or indictment from the government can hire expert talent, in the form of a tax or defense lawyer. A specialist who knows all the ins and outs can help tremendously, and many people do conduct successful defenses with their aid.

The big problem is for the person who doesn't know that he's being investigated, and who unwittingly helps the government by unwise or indiscreet actions.

"The police" is a convenient term that I'll use to apply to various levels of government and their law enforcement arms in this discussion. Whatever the purpose of a law enforcement agency, many of the investigative tools and techniques are the same. They don't all use them equally, for some are appropriate to certain situations and not to others. I intend to sketch briefly the techniques so you can understand them and make an informed judgement as to whether you're vulnerable to them. This will expose some of the otherwise hidden dangers inherent in what you may be doing.

Don't expect that "Big Brother" is watching you all the time. He simply doesn't have the manpower or the resources to watch everyone every moment. The main value of this chapter is to alert you to not only the technical means of privacy invasion, but the *forms of behavior* that arouse police interest, even though they're not illegal themselves.

The police often use both legal and illegal methods, sometimes in very imaginative ways. It's worth repeating that, although they won't use every method on you, these techniques are available to them, and you may wind up in their files by accident, because they're investigating someone with whom you came into contact.

Some of the techniques and equipment are classified, such as some of the computer equipment used by various branches of the government, and much of the rest, such as investigative techniques used by police agencies, are not general information. Let's build up a picture of what's available to the police and how they use it.

AUDIO SURVEILLANCE

This is commonly known as "bugging," and is a technique useful for intensive investigations. It requires a certain amount of manpower and a court order to gain access legally to premises in order to install a hidden transmitter.

"Bugging" is an old technique, dating from around the turn of the Century, and police have used it, sometimes indiscriminately, with and without court orders. This is a very sore point, and there have been Congressional investigations regarding illegal audio surveillance, both by local agencies and Federal ones, including the FBI and the Internal Revenue Service.

There are many methods of audio surveillance[1] and they don't all apply to you. If police interest in you is such that they actually bug you, it's time to look for a lawyer.

BLACK BAG JOBS

This refers to surreptitious entry, and again, can happen with or without a court order. This can be to install an electronic surveillance device, or to permit a physical search for evidence.

The problem of illegal entries by police has been with us for decades, and is with us today. Even the most respected agencies, such as the FBI, do it.[2] It's not enough to install alarms and high-security locks for protection. Police agencies employ experts at forced entry, and they're knowledgeable enough to defeat almost any system.[3] Even private investigators and amateurs have available information regarding the opening of locks.[4]

Formerly, tools for such entries were available only to locksmiths and police, but sources are now open to private investigators and, in fact, anyone else who has the modest amount of money required.[5]

BANK RECORDS AND TRANSACTIONS

Most bank records are computerized, but it's important to deal with them separately, because they pose special dangers. A cancelled check for a safe-deposit box rental, a Post Office box, a mail drop payment, or a private vault can provide an investigator with a valuable lead.

COMPUTER SEARCH

There are computerized files on almost everyone and everything, and they're becoming more comprehensive every day. There is a Federal privacy law, and a number of local ones, but in fact they don't stop the determined investigator. If high school students can penetrate sophisticated computers and gain access to the information in them, it's not too much to imagine that the police employ experts to tap into computers when they can't get a court order for the information they want.

A short list of some of the records available in computer memories includes: (airlines use computers, too — keep this in mind when planning a trip), car rental records, criminal records, tax files, bank records, including your savings and checking accounts, Social Security accounts, automobile registrations, drivers license records, and passports. Obviously, this list only gives a sampling, but it does provide the dimensions of the problem. Unless you were born and raised in the backwoods, with no birth certificate, never attended school, never were hospitalized, never were in the Armed Services, never had a drivers license or owned a car, never filed a tax return, never took a commercial flight, never took out a loan or had a bank account, and generally lived out of contact with civilization, you're in a computer somewhere.[6]

INFORMERS

Informers, or "snitches," are a traditional investigative tool. Many private individuals have knowledge that interests the police, and prying it out of them can be rewarding. Basically, there are several ways of developing informers:

(1) The person who snitches out of jealousy or revenge. Someone who has a personal dislike for you and knows of an illegal activity can inform the police.

(2) A co-conspirator is open to an offer of lesser charges or immunity if he provides information.

(3) A third party can be motivated by greed and rewarded by a payment, as in the "Silent Witness" program run by local police departments, and the "Turn In A Friend" program run by the Internal Revenue Service.

MAIL COVER

This little-known tool of the Postal Inspection Service is

available to all police agencies. The law states clearly that First Class mail may not be opened except with a court order, but there's nothing to prevent the Postal Inspectors from recording the return addresses of a target's mail, or to record the addresses on outgoing mail.

Because of a tradition of cooperation between police agencies, Postal Inspectors provide information to other agencies at all levels. Here's a list of possibilities:

- Mail covers of sexually-oriented publications to provide a suspect list for investigation of sex crimes.

- Covers of subscribers to para-military publications to develop a list of potential illegal firearms owners.

- Lists of subscribers to certain extreme political organizations and publications.

- Subscribers to gun magazines.

- Persons who order gun-related supplies by mail.

This is not to say that surreptitious opening of mail never happens without a court order. It does show, however, that it's not necessary to *open* an envelope to obtain damaging information about a person under investigation, or to develop a list of suspects.

TELEPHONE TAPS

Properly, this belongs under electronic and audio surveillance, but it's a special case, and deserves a special section.

The old days, when a police agent had to gain access to his target's telephone or wire to install a tap, are gone. With the introduction of the electronic switching system (ESS), it's possible to tap into any phone line from a central location. It's also possible to trace a call in seconds, something which formerly took several minutes at best.

Federal Government agencies, such as NSA, have computers which they use in computer-espionage work, which are capable of monitoring many telephone calls at once, scanning them and recognizing specific words programmed into them. This speeds up telephone line monitoring, and enhances detection of conversations about certain subjects which might interest investigators. That the government monitors telephone conversations is a wide-open secret, and not only in this country.

PUTTING IT TOGETHER

Let's take a hypothetical case, that of Mr. X, to see how he may be vulnerable to investigation. We'll assume that the police make use of computers to tie information together and narrow the range of investigation to suspects who offer maximum chances to them.

A mail cover of a political organization shows that Mr. X regularly gets literature from them. A computerized cross-check shows that he subscribes to several gun magazines. Another cross-check shows that he has ordered reloading tools, perfectly legally, by mail from several suppliers. His checking account (all checks are now microfilmed by law) shows that he makes regular contributions to an organization that promotes tax avoidance and evasion. He also has written checks to a private mail drop, a private storage vault, and to suppliers of plumbing equipment, in amounts that suggest he may be running a business on the side and salting away the profits without paying taxes on them. An investigator drives down his street to look at his house, and a comparison with his tax records suggests that his house is out of proportion to his income. Checking airline records, suggested by his credit card records, shows that he's taken several vacations that cost a good part of his declared income, so much that he's almost certainly a tax evader.

The picture that emerges is that of a politically extreme person, certainly armed and possibly dangerous. Even the most unimaginative investigator can see that there is justification for a careful audit of his tax return by the

Internal Revenue Service, and the possibility of a criminal prosecution.

This hypothetical case shows some of the dangers of carelessness in the underground economy. We have to see the picture in perspective, though. There are many people who subscribe to various magazines, or are members of political organizations of all complexions. Most of them are not tax evaders, at least not conspicuously. This means there's latitude for a few mistakes. Computer checks by the police aim not so much at finding individual names and actions, but at finding people who fit a "profile," a pattern of behavior which suggests they're serious violators.

This means a "hit" in one area is not as significant as fitting a pattern with hits in several areas, as we've seen in the case of Mr. X.

Entering the underground economy means more than just not declaring income. It also means being watchful, and not giving clues to the activity.

NOTES

1. *How to Avoid Electronic Eavesdropping and Privacy Invasion* by Anonymous, 1976, Investigator's Information Service, 806 S. Robertson Blvd., Los Angeles, CA, 90035. This semi-technical discussion of audio surveillance, including phone tapping, is oriented towards the person who wants to protect himself against it, and lists many techniques and devices useful for countering such intrusion.

2. *The FBI Nobody Knows,* Fred J. Cook, MacMillan Company, New York, 1964, pp. 28-31.

3. *The Big Brother Game,* Scott French, Lyle Stuart, 120 Enterprise Ave, Secaucus, NJ 07094, 1975, pp. 110-141.

4. *Locks, Picks, and Clicks,* anonymous, Diamondback Books, Phoenix, AZ, 1975. This book, although detailing methods dating from the 1940s, is still valuable because many locks from that era are still in use. This is just one of the many books available on the subject.

5. One company which sells by mail-order is: American Locksmith Service, PO Box 26, Culver City, CA 90232-0026. This company puts out a line which includes a master lockpicking kit in a small case, and "Slim Jims," tools for opening car doors without keys.

6. *The Big Brother Game*, pp. 163-183.

18

Winning Against the IRS

Unfortunately, it's true that you can't win a confrontation with the IRS. They have the law and the manpower on their side. If you stand up to fight them, they'll knock you flat.

Is this always true, though? Aren't there some instances of people who have fought and won?

Yes, there are, but it takes a lot of money and a good lawyer, and the risks are great. You don't have to win in court, though. There are other ways of winning.

As noted before, keeping a low profile is one way of winning. *The best way to win is not to have to fight,* and if the IRS never sees you, it can't amputate what's yours, and you win.

Part of keeping a low profile is being one of many. Small businessmen, who don't have the power and influence to get for themselves the special tax breaks the rich have, generally under-report their incomes by fifteen or twenty percent.[1]

This costs the government billions of dollars. In its "official" figures, the IRS tries to underplay this because it doesn't want it let out how truly inefficient it is.[2]

These figures are frightening to the people in the government. Money isn't the only problem — widespread disobedience of the tax laws is another. A Federal judge in

Montana stated that if one thousand people in that state were to file falsified withholding forms, it could "destroy" the system.[3] In that case, the defendants were five men. Probably, they were the only five who'd been caught!

There are two ways of interpreting such news. One is the "rotten apple" interpretation, in which we consider the ones being prosecuted as just a few rotten apples in the barrel. The other is the "tip of the iceberg" theory, which leads us to believe that those who have surfaced are only a few of the many who have gimmicked their W-4s.

It doesn't take much insight to decide which is the correct interpretation. The evidence is overwhelming that many more people are involved in tax avoidance than the IRS wants to admit. Despite its propaganda line that tax cheaters are just a few isolated criminals, it's evident that there are many.

Consider just one category — migrant workers. There's reason to believe that tens of thousands of them file false W-4s.[4] Some of these are in the construction industry, and others are farm workers.

The huge number of violators results in saturation of the IRS. It simply does not have enough investigators to audit every tax return filed by every self-employed person in the country, nor to track down every person who has filed a falsified W-4.

Despite threats of prosecution by the IRS, the chances of them catching violators are slim, for other reasons. First is the complexity of the legal system. It's possible, by pleading "not guilty," to delay trial and sentencing for months or years, even if one is actually guilty. Next is the limited manpower of the various public prosecutors. Even in criminal cases, very few defendants come to trial. Most cases resolve themselves by plea agreements.

The major task for which the IRS exists is to collect money. If the IRS catches a middle-class homeowner short on his taxes and he is unwilling to pay up, it can slam the iron fist of repression down on him and seize his house, his car and other property, attach his wages, and confiscate his bank accounts.

Possibly one of the biggest secrets the IRS keeps is that *it can do almost nothing against tax evaders who are poor.* They own only the clothing on their backs, or perhaps a second-hand car. The car is probably not paid up, which gives the IRS very little to grab.

The IRS justifies its existence by collecting money from taxpayers. Rumor has it that a tax examiner has to fulfill a quota of one hundred dollars per hour to satisfy his supervisors. In that regard, it simply doesn't pay for the IRS bloodhounds to chase down the lowest economic class of tax evaders, because they can't squeeze the money out of them. We see, therefore, that poverty or near-poverty is a protection against the IRS examiners, and it hits them right where they live.

Consequently, it is possible to "win" against the IRS, under certain circumstances. "Winning" does not necessarily mean open defiance, but just getting away with not paying taxes.

NOTES

1. Martin Larson's Best, Spotlight, Washington, D.C., Liberty Lobby, 1982, p. 15. Many simply don't get caught, for two reasons: they're too careful, and there are too many of them.
2. *Ibid.*, p. 15, Column 2, estimates a low of fifty billion and a high of eighty.
3. *Ibid.*, p. 18.
4. *Ibid.*, p. 31.

19

More Underground Economy People

Ron is a police sergeant, the commander of his department's SWAT Team. Unlike other members of the team, and the force in general, Ron is very frugal and keeps his eyes open for easy ways to pick up extra money. He picks up the empty cartridges after each session of firing range practice for sale to reloaders, or to use in barter. Recently, he traded 7,500 fired .223 cases to a gun dealer for a new .308 caliber rifle. None of this ever gets reported on Ron's tax returns.

Daryl lives in Arizona, and his four-wheeler is well-equipped with a winch, several five-gallon cans of gasoline, containers of water, rope, shovels, a comprehensive tool kit, and a first aid kit. On weekends, he goes out tooling around in the desert, just driving around, exploring, camping, shooting, and generally having fun. Sometimes he takes a girl or buddy along. Often, he runs across people who are stranded for lack of gas, oil, or water, or are stuck in the sand and can't get out. Daryl is glad to help them out, and can usually pay for his weekend, or more, by towing, and selling gas, oil and water. Daryl has a very helpful attitude, and people show their appreciation in a monetary way. He doesn't report any of the money he makes this way.

Sandy buys and restores antique cameras and sells them to collectors. A camera collector herself, she knows what to look for when she visits garage sales, second hand stores and antique shops. Sometimes Sandy will place a small ad in her local shopping guide, and will put 3 x 5 cards on local bulletin boards. In this way, she sometimes is able to purchase old cameras that people have had tucked away in their attics for years — often needing only cleaning, and not repairs. Sandy also buys old cameras that do not work, because she knows she can get them cheap, and if she can't fix them, they will be useful for parts, since new parts for these old cameras are not being made anymore. Before she was married, her camera collecting was strictly a hobby for Sandy, but now with one child in the family, and another on the way, she has turned her hobby into a modestly profitable business. Sandy sells most of her restored cameras for cash at flea markets, so keeping the income off the books is no problem for her. Sandy has built up a list of collectors and their specialities, and can often get sales just by making a phone call.

Bonnie was an office worker all her life, and retired from the civil service after heading the payroll section of her agency. She knows her way around bookkeeping and after retiring, she put her skills to work in an underground part-time business. Through a neighbor, she met Danny, who was struggling to set up a landscaping business. He was good at his work, but not enthusiastic about all the paperwork that even a small business requires. Bonnie began handling Danny's paperwork, collecting his invoices, paying his bills, making out his payroll, and acting as an answering service for his calls when he was out on a job. She allowed him to use her home as the mailing address for his business, which was a convenience for her, since then Danny's bills and checks came right into her mailbox. Danny pays her a modest monthly salary for these services, and pays her in cash. He does not take a deduction on his income tax for her salary, but does "adjust" his books in other ways to absorb the expense. Bonnie has no other clients and isn't looking for any. Danny's work keeps her exactly as busy as she wants to be, and the money is a nice supplement to her pension. She has never reported any of the money from her little sideline.

Jesse is a mechanic for a Datsun dealership, but also does weekend work for private customers. He works both in his backyard and at customers' homes, and has no trouble keeping busy. His regular boss does not object, because he sells and services only Datsuns, and Jesse confines his moonlighting to other makes. With new car prices sky high and not about to come down, Americans are keeping their old cars longer, which creates an increasing market for skilled repairs. Jesse advertises by word-of-mouth, and can easily undercut the prices of the aboveground repair shops which have to have licenses and pay taxes, as well as obey zoning and other restrictive ordinances. Jesse had most of his own tools when he started his little sideline, and buys additional ones with the income from his business. Most of his customers pay in cash, so hiding the income is no problem. When he gets a check, Jesse simply signs it over to an auto supply store, for parts and supplies. Jesse has been doing this for years and sometimes his weekend income exceeds what he makes on his regular job.

Carmen runs a little off-the-books business writing letters for people who cannot read or write very well. The only equipment she needs is a typewriter, and all her advertising is done on community bulletin boards. Her ad, on a 3 x 5 card, reads like this: LETTERS WRITTEN. DO YOU NEED TO SEND A LETTER TO A FRIEND, OR FAMILY MEMBER? DO YOU NEED TO SEND A LETTER TO THE GOVERNMENT, OR TO A COMPANY? LET ME HELP YOU WRITE IT. YOU GET A NEATLY TYPED LETTER, SAYING EXACTLY WHAT YOU WANT TO SAY, AT LOW COST. Her price and telephone number are also listed on the card. Since her fee is so small, all her clients pay her in cash. She has never reported any of this income.

Judy has an expensive electric typewriter and uses it to earn extra money, tax-free. Married to a deputy sheriff, with two children, she finds it hard to balance the household budget on her husband's salary alone. They live in a college town, where there are many students who need someone to type their handwritten manuscripts, since most instructors now require all term papers to be typewritten. Judy advertises by placing 3 x 5 cards on campus bulletin boards, and this brings her all the business she can handle. She works out of her home, which is near the campus, so the students deliver their papers to her, and come back to pick them up. This enables Judy to take care of her household and avoids having to leave the children alone. With no overhead, she can afford to charge less than commercial typing services. The students always pay her in cash. If one of them tries to give her a check, she just tells them, "Look, I have kids to take care of, and don't have time to run to the bank. Can't you cash your own check at the bank and just bring me the money?" This has worked every time so far.

Janet runs a telephone answering service out of her apartment. She doesn't patch into her client's phones, just has them list her number on their business cards and invoices for their customers to call when they get no answer at the regular numbers. Her clients are mainly one-man business owners, such as electricians and plumbers, who are often out on business and unable to answer their phones. Janet has four phones in her apartment, in four different names. She doesn't want the phone company to know she is running a commercial service, both to save money and to avoid the awkward questions that can produce. She doesn't want to be listed in the yellow pages, which would be a sure tip-off to prowling government tax agents. Janet has one helper, a friend on ADC who comes in four hours a day so Janet can have some time off for shopping, etc. Janet is on ADC herself and doesn't want any on-the-books earnings, so she just doesn't report any of her income. When she is paid by check, as she usually is, she just simply deposits the checks in her personal account. She hasn't been caught yet, and does not expect to be. That extra income means a lot to her and her four year old daughter.

Bill works as a maintenance man for his city government. After hours and on weekends, he runs his own small air conditioning business, off the books, using the city's tools. His supervisor doesn't know about Bill's little sideline, and it isn't hard for Bill to keep it to himself. When his customers pay him in cash, he simply pockets it. When he receives checks, he endorses them over to his supplier, with whom he has done business for many years and who is quite willing to help out a client. The supplier suspects exactly what is going on, but is willing to accept second party checks from Bill because he knows Bill will make good on any that bounce, and also because he knows that Bill would take his business to another supplier if he wasn't willing to do this little favor for Bill. Bill advertises only by word-of-mouth, and services a small handful of office and apartment buildings. Like most moonlighters, he gets and keeps clients because he charges less than his above-ground competitors. He keeps his client list small enough so that he can do all the work himself, and thus avoids the paperwork, hassles, and expenses of hiring employees.

Rudy runs an after-hours club. While the laws in his city are strict governing the operation of bars open to the public, private clubs can do as they please. Rudy does not allow the general public in. Anyone seeking admission must join the "club" by paying a nominal fee, and get a membership card. The card entitles the bearer to service at the bar and to bring as many guests as he wishes. It's a cash business. Rudy rented an old building on a side street. He runs the club on weekends only, and doesn't need a liquor license since it is a private club. It is a cash business, and Rudy doesn't bother to report any of the income. He has some experience bartending, as does his wife, who helps him in the club. Rudy's is a very low-profile operation, and his only advertising is word-of-mouth. Rudy has run his after-hours club for three years now, and the income is now equal to what he makes on his regular job.

Pat is a confirmed gun nut, and so are most of his friends. Like Pat, many of them cast their own bullets, and complain about the high price of bullet lubricant. Pat mixes his own, in gallon batches, and makes money on the side by selling or bartering bullet lube with his reloading friends. Bullet lube is not covered by any firearms laws, so Pat is in the clear there. His friends pay him with cash or barter, so Pat doesn't report any of this income. Some of his friends are doing similar things, and none of them ever expects to be caught.

Maria is an underground cleaning lady. She has a list of clients, acquired over the years by word-of-mouth, and spends her workdays scurrying from one apartment to another, taking the subway or bus, or walking if the distance permits it. She tries to arrange her schedule so she services clients close to each other on the same days, thus saving time as well as subway and bus fares. Her clients usually leave her fee on the table, and tell Maria to help herself to the leftovers in the refrigerator for lunch. Maria's clients are affluent business couples, so she eats well, and often is able to take some of the leftovers home with her in her shopping bag, for supper. Another fringe benefit Maria gets is when her clients discard clothing which has gone out of style. Maria's clients like her and usually offer her first choice before donating the clothing to the Salvation Army. All her clients pay her in cash, and do not withhold any taxes. Maria does not report any of her income.

20

Making the Most of Receipts

Receipts are the heart of any deductions you claim on your tax return. The Internal Revenue Service demands substantiation for any deductions, and this usually means having a piece of paper to show.

Receipts take many forms, sometimes being just scrawled notes, but they look better if they're printed, preferably on a cash register. A hand-written receipt on a printed form will also do very well.

An interesting thing about receipts is that there's no standard format, either by custom or by law. There 's no law requiring that a receipt be itemized, or that it list the nature of the item in the transaction, although many do.

The following example shows how manipulation of receipts will often cover a person's need, whether regarding tax deductions or collecting on an expense account.

Nick took a trip to Atlanta for his company. He was alloted a per diem, and would be reimbursed for anything above that, if he could turn in a receipt. He wanted to make a side-trip to see an old friend, but knew his company would not reimburse him for this personal business. He took the trip anyway, and his friend treated Nick to dinner at a restaurant called "The Tillerman." When the check came and his friend paid, Nick noticed that the stub, which served as a receipt for those who had expense accounts, did not state the nature of the establishment, and furthermore the amount was blank. Restaurants often avoid filling in the amount, as the proprietors know this is an accomodation to the businessman who wants to falsify his accounts, and will indirectly bring in a few extra customers. Nick asked his friend for the stub, filling in an amount that would cover his extra air fare, and passed it off as a motel receipt when he turned in his expense sheet.

It's sometimes possible to produce duplication of receipts to pad the expense column. Jack had to mail several items, and was able to deduct the postage as a business expense. One of the items had to go by Express Mail. At the Post Office, he made out the four-part Express Mail form and got back his copy, which he would use as a cash receipt. As he was mailing other items too, he asked the clerk for another receipt to cover the entire amount, which the clerk willingly gave him. This, he paid by check. Now Jack had a receipt for a different amount, paid by check. Jack had his cake and ate it, too.

Warren, a plumber, often bought at a hardware store where his friend was manager. His friend would give him discounts, but write up a receipt for the full list prices. Warren usually paid in cash. For large purchases, he paid by check. His friend would provide a receipt for the items at list, and Warren would write a check for the discounted price, plus sales tax. The receipts were undated, being simply strips torn off an adding machine, and with the store's stamp at the top. This made it possible for Warren to list his cancelled check as an expense, and also deduct the receipt as a cash paid out, as the amounts differed and there was no date on the receipt to bring suspicion.

For these methods to work, the receipt and the check should show different amounts, which an auditor will take to mean that they cover different purchases. This will help even if they're dated the same day, as many businessmen make more than one purchase from the same source on the same day. Having the receipt undated helps even more.

Putting on your own dates with a date stamp can be worthwhile, too.

Using cancelled checks as receipts is a conventional and accepted practice. There are many businesses which don't issue receipts, and this means the cancelled check is often the only record of an expense being paid. It's conventional to "vouch" a cancelled check, to staple it to an invoice or purchase order, but many small businesses simply don't do this, as there's no legal requirement for it. This omission lends itself very well to doubling up on checks and receipts, because it makes the transactions virtually untraceable. There are several ways to do this, in addition to the examples cited above.

(1) The businessman post-dates his checks by a day or two, on the pretext that he's waiting for a deposit to clear. This yields him a reciept and a check with different dates, which makes it hard to prove they're for one and the same expense.

One possible problem arises if the supplier writes on the receipt both the date and the check number. An examiner, finding this correlation, will easily disallow the extra deduction. If this happens, the taxpayer can simply claim he made a mistake, and forgot to vouch the two. This is an easily acceptable excuse.

(2) Another way is to write the check for a different amount. One excuse to tell the supplier is that there's not enough money in the checking account to cover the bill, and to obtain his agreement to partial payment on that day, and the balance a couple of days later. Most suppliers, if they have regular dealings with the customer and have done this in the past, will allow it. We now have two checks, neither of which matches the amount of the receipt, and only a very astute examiner would catch this subtle point and discover the doubling-up.

(3) Yet another way is to write a check for more than the receipt, asking for the difference in cash on the pretext of being short of pocket money. This has a two-fold effect. First, it obscures the relationship between the receipt and

the check, enabling doubling-up on deductions. The second effect is to provide money for personal use, yet have it officially listed as a business expense.

Making the most of receipts takes judgement and discretion. Some may be tempted to forge receipts, or to alter genuine ones. This is foolish, because with a little bad luck, it provides documentation of intent to commit fraud. There are exceptions to every rule, though, and let's look at the ones for this.

The first point is to take the overall view. It's possible by injudicious use of deductions, to claim expenses which are way out of line. A tax examiner auditing a return will immediately notice if claimed business expenses are so great they don't leave the claimant enough to live on.

IRS auditors have guidelines, tables of average deductions and expenses for various categories of businesses. This gives them clues when claimed deductions are questionable, and a lever with which to probe further. Therefore, any deductions must be approximately within average guidelines, in order not to attract attention.

We have to note several characteristics of receipts, because there are some pitfalls for the unwary. First, they must be credible. A receipt from a liquor store can pose problems, if the store name and/or type of business shows on it. It will then be necessary to "backstop" the receipt by claiming "entertainment" deductions, which means that it's essential to show a need for entertaining clients, or at least that it was necessary to give liquor as Christmas presents to some clients. Fortunately, this is common practice in many businesses, and the only point to watch is that the date on the receipt, if there is one, should be shortly before Christmas.

Another important point is the printing on the receipt. Some department stores code their receipts with a key for each department. This is for their internal accounting purposes, not to help the IRS, but a sophisticated IRS examiner can make use of this if he knows the codes, which are not secret and easy to find out with a phone call. Some department stores print the appropriate letter codes right on their price tags, for the cashier's benefit, and an IRS examiner can simply walk in and note the type of merchandise sold under each letter code.

For example, if a businessman buys liquor at such a store, and each department has its own letter code, this can trip him up. If he writes on the receipt, "tools," and the slip has the letter "H" alongside the amount, it will cause him a problem if "H" stands for "liquor." Perhaps the hardware department has the letter "P," and the businessman must be aware of this to make his receipts internally consistent.

One dangerous practice is to forge receipts. The risk depends on the method. Some try to alter a receipt, something which can be hard to do. A cash register receipt is almost impossible to alter, because changing the amount will mean inserting another printed number, and this is very difficult. A hand-written receipt is easier to alter, at least to pass a superficial examination. It's possible to change a figure from $50.00 to $150.00 by inserting a numeral "1" before the "50.00," but only if the numbers aren't closely spaced. This does, however, bring up several problems.

The type of writing must be the same. The ink and the type of pen must match, as a start. Under close scrutiny, by a questioned documents examiner, any difference in type of ink can show up, even though they may seem to be the same color. Questioned documents examiners have various ways of differentiating inks, such as photographing them through filters, and using ultra-violet and infra-red light.

Actually, few receipts turned in to the IRS ever wind up on the desk of a questioned documents examiner, but this is a possibility which the businessman must keep in mind, because there are easier ways of fudging receipts.

Outright forgery is safer, because it does not present any incriminating evidence on its face. Businessmen who have dealings with other businesses have many opportunities to pick up copies of invoices from them. It's as easy as taking a few off a pile on a desk. The preferable type of invoice is the one that is not serially-numbered, because this makes it harder to disprove. Serially-numbered invoices are always correlated with other documents in the company's internal accounting. An invoice for a service call, for example, will lead to a listing on a service man's route sheet, where he lists all the calls he makes each day. It's usually one component of a multi-part form, with several duplicates floating around in the company's files.

An invoice for a shipment will correlate with a shipping memo, a purchase or work order, and other documents. A persistent investigation will reveal any such claims that are not backed up in the company's files.

Fortunately for the small businessman, many companies don't have rigorous internal accounting methods, and this precludes the IRS examiner's proving a claim spurious by failing to find a trace. Many receipts are written on cheap pads from the local stationary store, and don't have serial numbers. Many small businessmen don't bother to have invoices with their company names printed. This makes forgery easy.

This is very important as a safeguard against prosecution. *An IRS examiner will be mainly interested in disallowing deductions, not starting a prosecution.* Failing to find substantiation of a deduction simply means that he disallows the deduction. On the other hand, providing him with a forged document that he can trace and prove false, gives him proof that there was a deliberate attempt to defraud the government, and this can lead to serious consequences.

This is a critical point. Failure to list income can be "explained" as "forgetting," and many examiners will accept this, although they suspect it's an outright lie, because they're more interested in collecting tax money than spending public funds to keep a delinquent taxpayer in prison. It's also possible to explain many bookkeeping irregularities as "errors," but an outright forgery is beyond explanation. It's documentary, prima-facie evidence which many examiners will not ignore.

The sophisticated businessman keeps any and all receipts he comes across, saving them in a shoe-box for convenience, because he knows he may need one or more of them to help him with his deductions. Many will be unsuitable, for various reasons. Some will be coded, showing the department of the store, which will perhaps cause him difficulty in assigning the deduction. Many will have the store or business's name printed, which again can make it difficult to use them for deductions. Supermarkets, for example, don't carry many items that are needed to run a business, which makes this category of receipt questionable. Not always though: Dave owned a block of apartments, and did all his shopping at a department store which had a supermarket as well as other departments. He saved all his receipts, because at the time, this department store did not code its receipts, having only the store name and the prices printed on the cash register receipts. This enabled Dave to include food and liquor purchases in his "business expenses," claiming them as "paint," "hardware," and other supplies he used for maintaining the property.

One serious limitation comes from dated receipts. Each year's tax form allows listing only that year's expenses, and many receipts from previous years become useless.

Sometimes we find a group effort. Like-minded businessmen occasionally hold "tax parties." One who needs receipts will phone several others whom he knows save their receipts as he does, and invite them to a party. The host provides the liquor, and the guests bring their shoe-boxes full of receipts. The host sorts through them, culling the ones which he can use. This often works as a round-robin, with several parties held around tax time, as the participants help each other beat the tax bite.

We see from the above that the small taxpayer is not utterly helpless before the IRS. While big businessmen have their sophisticated methods of avoiding paying taxes, the small taxpayer can defend himself too, if he uses his brain and knows how to make the most of his receipts.

21

Backstopping: A Vital Point

The term "backstopping" is one we hardly ever see outside the professional literature, yet it's vital to understand it and to use the concept, because otherwise we risk serious problems.

Various books have dealt with forgery of various sorts. It's possible to forge everything from a birth certificate to a drivers license, complete with color photograph. However, a totally forged drivers license, no matter how perfect, will not stand up to examination, for a very good reason. If the person carrying it is stopped by a police officer, even for a minor traffic violation, the routine radio check with the state drivers license bureau will disclose that there is no record of that license being issued. If the forgery is an adaptation of a license already issued, with the name and photograph changed, it will be immediately apparent that the records show it as issued in another name.

The point is clear: *there have to be supporting documents to "backstop" the forgery,* and they have to be consistent with the forgery in order not to arouse suspicion. This is relevant to people who try to forge documents to support an effort to evade taxes. Sometimes, a lack of backstopping will reveal the forgery during an investigation, even though the forgery itself may be perfect.

An example is an invoice from a non-existent company. It's easy to have anything printed, including invoices. However, a suspicious Internal Revenue Agent who decides to make a phone call will soon find that such an invoice is spurious. It doesn't necessarily take a phone call. A quick check of the yellow pages will show no listing for the spurious company, and this will prompt a more intensive investigation.

One device that will reduce the risk is to search through subsequent editions of the yellow pages for companies that have gone out of business. Printing paperwork purporting to be from one of these companies is fairly safe, as it's not easy at all to check it out, even for the most suspicious investigator. Verification would require tracing the former executives of the defunct company, and trying to obtain a sample of their paperwork, which may have been destroyed. Even then, if the forgery isn't clumsy, it may remain unprovable.

Any employee of the defunct company might be able to say that the company letterhead or logo did not look like the forgery, if the forger did not take the elementary precautions of reproducing the genuine article. However, asking any former owner or employee to remember whether a single invoice was actually issued is beyond reason, especially if the records no longer exist.

As we've seen, it's possible to "lift" some invoices from a company while visiting. Often, it's as easy as taking a few off a pile on a desk. Depending on how involved the company's accounting system is, this can be a help or a time-bomb, waiting to explode upon the slightest investigation. If the invoices are serially numbered, it will be impossible to produce anything that will stand up to even the most casual investigation. Unless the IRS examiner accepts it at face value, tracing the invoice to prove it is a fake will be very easy, unless the company no longer exists and the records have been destroyed.

Having an accomplice inside the company will help, but

even with this, the built-in controls of the accounting system may make backstopping the invoice difficult or impossible. It's always possible to insert a copy of the invoice, and even a supporting purchase order and shipping records, but at the yearly internal audit the discrepancy will show up because the internal auditor will find no record of payment to match with the other paperwork.

One significant exception is a going concern that has recently had its records destroyed by fire. This doesn't happen often enough to make it a serious prospect. Although there are many fires each year in American cities, the coincidence of having one at a company whose paperwork might be useful for supporting tax deductions is not very common, and in any event, it would first be wise to find out if the company normally microfilms its paperwork to guard against such an eventuality.

We can see, therefore, that getting paperwork to support claimed deductions is not as easy as it might seem, and the opportunities are limited. Certain conditions are absolute disqualifiers, and merely provide a government prosecutor with documentary evidence of intent to defraud if there's the slightest investigation.

With all this, there's a lot of paperwork that lends itself to it, such as the following:

(1) Cash register receipts.

(2) Invoices without serial numbers.

(3) Restaurant receipts and stubs, especially if they're not numbered and the cashier fails to fill in the amount.

(4) Cancelled checks, especially if they duplicate actual payments. These are often very safe to use.

(5) Documents issued by a business which has a friendly owner, who is willing to help actively and falsify his records in a way that will stand up to investigation.

We see that backstopping is not necessary for many pieces of paperwork, because they're not part of a strictly controlled system. However, failure to backstop when it's required can lead to disaster.

22

The "Tax Party"

Often, people are caught in the audit net the IRS sets out. Sometimes, it's because of stupidity. Other times, it's just the normal course of affairs, as in the case of anyone who is self-employed and in the fifty-thousand dollar income bracket, the one to which the IRS pays closest attention.

What can the individual do to protect himself? Let's listen to "Jerry," a self-employed printer who has had a lot of experience with the IRS. Jerry understands the way the world really works, and is realistic. He doesn't try any bizarre antics, either to earn money or to keep it — just common-sense measures that enable him to keep a greater share of his profits than the IRS would like. He says:

"I've been audited each year for the last three years. The IRS knows I'm self-employed, which gives me the opportunity to play a few games with them, and they do not like that at all. I know they can only audit me once a year, so I take advantage of that. The IRS man has to show something for his audit, and I let him have something. In return, I get something.

"When I get a notice that they want me for an audit, I call all my friends, and hold a tax party. They bring all the cash register receipts, invoices, and other paperwork they can, and we have a big party while doing it. We all have our tax parties, and help each other out.

"When the time comes for me to see the IRS man, I work it one of two ways. I let him question the deductions he wants, and watch while he takes them off my return. Say he takes off five hundred dollars' worth. Then I pull out my envelope and say:

"'While I was getting my papers together for this meeting, I ran across another five hundred dollars' worth of deductions I'd forgotten to include. Here they are.'

"This puts me back on the track again. Sometimes, though, I work it differently, because I know the poor guy has to meet his productivity quota, and I don't try to stonewall him. He takes off the amount of deductions he wants, and I write a check to cover the additional taxes. Then I file an amended return, a Form 1040-X, adding the new deductions based on what I collected at the tax party. I send this in, and the IRS sends me a refund.

"Because I'm a printer, I get a chance to obtain a lot of forms and invoices that wouldn't otherwise come my way. I do a lot of jobs for businesses, and I keep a few of each one I print. I also have a crackerjack typesetter who'll fix me up with anything I ask. When I need some invoices to support some deductions, I pull them out of my file of blanks and fill them in, or have a friend fill them in. I have a PAID stamp, and I stamp them, and that's that.

"The reason this works is the IRS people are paper-happy. They don't care what it is or where it comes from, as long as it's on a piece of paper. It's a cover-your-ass thing, and it doesn't matter who is being audited. The only thing that counts is that piece of paper. They never check it out.

"This is why any sort of receipt works for me. I can have a receipt from a motel where I took a broad, and include it as business entertainment. I keep my supermarket receipts — maybe they'll be good for something, someday. Just about anything at all can go, if you use a little imagination with it. It's hard to believe what you can get away with. Any piece of paper will do.

"A friend of mine owns a bunch of rental properties. He has to maintain them, and in doing this he gets a lot of receipts from plumbers, electricians, and hardware stores. The IRS doesn't know whether the receipt is for work on his personal house or his rentals. The receipt doesn't give the address of the property. Hell, he even goes and saves the receipt when he buys liquor at the supermarket. The receipt doesn't say "Liquor Department," not where he buys it. He then marks it as "faucet" or something like that, and turns it in.

"It's surprising what you can get away with, but if you stop to think about it, you see how hard it is for the IRS to prove certain things. They can subpoena your bank records, and ask you to document every deduction. What if they question some of the pieces of paper you turn in? Can they go around to every supplier involved, and ask if the paper is legitimate? Say it's a supermarket receipt. Can they go to the supermarket, and ask the checkout girl if a receipt she punched out six months ago was for lightbulbs or for liquor? If it's something from a hardware store, a box of nails or screws, can they track down where you put every screw, to make sure they went for business use and not personal? No way!"

This is a refreshing point of view from a successful businessman who faces the IRS without anxiety, because he knows what works and what doesn't work.

Jerry is an above-ground businessman who has an underground side. His business gives him the "cover" he needs for his other activities, which include not only the extra deductions we've seen, but also a bit of "skimming."

"The guy who put in my pool, he wanted to do it under the table, and so did I. We worked it out. There was no paperwork at all. First, I paid him cash, but also gave him a trade-out. I got him five-hundred dollars' worth of printing, letterheads, envelopes, invoices, and such, and he took this as part payment. He gave me a nice discount for cash, and that resulted in my getting the pool half-price.

120

"I got a new air conditioner put in with no money at all changing hands. First, I paid for part of it in printing for the guy. Next, I had another customer who wanted to pay me for a job with a solar unit, which his company makes. I didn't want the unit, but I wondered if the air conditioning man might be interested. He looked at the set-up, and decided that he could sell it to another customer of his, and get paid for the installation, too. He took it, and that's how I got my air conditioner for nothing."

It helps to be a middleman, and to have lots of contacts. Contacts are the key to the sort of barter deals that Jerry uses, and also the key to cooperative acquisition of paperwork, as we've seen. With the right approach, it's possible to handle the tax problem without fear.

23

Pass It On!

If you're earning or saving money by using underground techniques, it will help you, both directly and indirectly, to pass on some of the benefits by getting others in on it. This doesn't mean talking about it openly, revealing your clever money-making methods — it means seeking co-conspirators in safe ways to beat the tax structure.

Co-opting others is both easy and profitable. Every tax dollar retained hurts the IRS, and helps the cause. Some practical ways to pass it on are:

■ Whenever you buy something from a local merchant, try to get a discount for cash. In an era when many people use credit cards, a cash sale pays off. In some cases, you don't have to ask. Many gas stations offer a discount, about four cents per gallon, for cash buyers. This is a healthy practice in two ways. It discourages the use of credit cards, which are simply a means of getting people to pay interest when they don't need to. It also lays the way open to the small businessman, the gas station operator, to skim off some of his income.

If you have to buy a tire or other hard goods at a gas station, ask the operator for the same deal he offers on gas. There's an incentive for him to cooperate with you, as the credit company or bank charges him for accepting the cards, "discounting" his invoices by four or five percent before paying him.

This doesn't work with large outlets, as a rule. They have "policy," and the clerks are not authorized to offer you any breaks beyond what the store allows, nor to make special "deals."

■ Seek out additional sources of supplies. Sometimes, it's possible to contact a wholesaler, and work out quantity or cash discounts. Remember, the more discount, the less sales tax.

■ Try to work barter when and wherever you can. You can do this at work, as well as in your personal life. Taking it out in trade is a common business practice, and it's even better if the exchange stays under the table.

If you're already in business for yourself, you have more latitude in taking the initiative. Canvass your accounts to find prospects of trade-outs or barter. Offer discounts for cash to those you know well. Get to know all your accounts better, so they'll give you hints on how they feel about taxes.

Paying cash is the first step. Not using legal tender is the next. It helps to participate in, and encourage, this method of exchange whenever possible.

Think of your friends and neighbors, and their occupations. Do any of them do anything that you might need? Plan how to approach them. If you have a skill or a product which you can exchange for what they offer, you'll have a way to open the door.

Nibbling away at the system, a small bite at a time, will build up a network of co-conspirators that will undermine it in your area. This depends on personal contacts, not oratory.

CO-OPTION

It seems contradictory, but keeping a low profile and spreading Guerrilla Capitalism around are not mutually exclusive. The basic principle is co-opting people into the fold.

Idle talk, bragging about your exploits, can lead to exposure. The government co-opts, too, with various informer programs.

For conversion to the cause, you need to show the person whom you're converting how he stands to gain. The best way to start is with a very limited move. A trade-out, or a cash payment, is a modest start. Once he realizes that the tax bite is an evil he can evade, he'll be more willing. As a participant, he's less likely to turn you in for a reward. This leads us to complicity.

Complicity means that the other party is equally guilty. Although we have little regard for the IRS, it still has its laws and rules which it can enforce. Complicity means drawing in the other party so that he has as much to lose as you do from disclosure.

FINDING YOUR PROSPECTS

A good starting point, even if there's no immediate opportunity to propose a trade-out, is when a friend complains about taxes, or inflation, or other economic ills. This is an opening for a discussion of practical measures to cope with these problems.

If you're a sympathetic person, willing to listen rather than pushing to talk, you'll have an advantage in recruiting people. Anyone who can offer understanding and quiet advice can make a good impression. The one who comes across as a fanatic operates with a handicap, as we have more than our share of political extremists and other kooks in this country, and most people, who occupy the middle ground, tend to be wary of these.

This technique works best in a one-to-one setting. Talking politics or economics in a group, especially if it takes place in a bar or at a party, can provoke long-winded and acrimonious discussions that don't settle anything.

Work towards limited goals. Rome wasn't built in a day, and neither was the "system." Don't strive for an enthusiastic convert the first time. Let him dip his toes in the water first, then get his feet wet.

Play it cool, take it slow, and you'll spread the word.

24

Recommended Reading

This continues the "Recommended Reading" list in *Guerrilla Capitalism: How To Practice Free Enterprise In An Unfree Economy.*

THE UNDERGROUND ECONOMY

Criminal Russia: Essays on Crime in the Soviet Union, by Valery Chalidze. 1977, Random House, New York. Revealing book on crime in the Soviet Union, with a 30 page chapter on "Private Enterprise."

Guerrilla Capitalism: How To Practice Free Enterprise in an Unfree Economy, by Adam Cash. 1984, Loompanics Unlimited, PO Box 1197, Port Townsend, WA 98368. My previous book on the Underground Economy. Maybe I am not an impartial evaluator, but this is the single best book ever written on the subject.

The Household Economy, by Scott Burns. 1975, Beacon Press, Boston. Fascinating and radical book detailing why the household economy is the true free enterprise system, and not the industrial economy. Even advocates the elimination of "money!"

The Inmate Economy, by David B. Kalinich. 1980, D.C. Heath and Company, Lexington, MA. How the inmates of Jackson (Michigan) Prison deal in contraband, in spite of living in an environment of total control.

Inside The Underground Economy, by Jerome Tuccille. 1982, Signet Books. A good book on both the Underground Economy and the aboveground tax protest movement.

Loompanics' Greatest Hits. 1984, Loompanics Unlimited, PO Box 1197, Port Townsend, WA 98368. Collection of articles from the Loompanics Unlimited Book Catalog, including several on taxes and the underground economy.

The Organization of Illegal Markets: An Economic Analysis, by Peter Reuter. 1986, Loompanics Unlimited, PO Box 1197, Port Townsend, WA 98368. Shows that illegal markets are run by a large number of small-scale entrepreneurs, rather than "The Mafia."

The §7201 Report on Tax Evasion. PO Box 165, Mt. Kisco, NY 10549. Newsletter on tax evasion, from a mostly negative point of view, published by a constitutional lawyer.

Taxation: An International Perspective, edited by Walter Block and Michael Walker. 1984, The Fraser Institute, 626 Bute St., Vancouver, BC, Canada V6E 3M1. Scholarly book on the tax systems of nine countries, and how high taxes have resulted in the emergence of an underground economy in each country.

STARTING NEW BUSINESSES
AND MOONLIGHTING

Beat The Racetrack, by William T. Ziemba and Donald B. Hausch. 1984, Harcourt Brace Jovanovich, Orlando, FL.

Good book on winning at the race track, which does not require use of a microcomputer.

Blackbelt In Blackjack, by Arnold Snyder. 1983, RGE, 2000 Center St. #1067, Berkeley, CA 94704. Good book on winning at casino blackjack.

Employing Family Members In Your Business: A Tax Bonanza!, W. Charles Blair and John K. McGill. 1983, Taxwise Publications Inc., Suite 1300-Charlotte Plaza Bldg., 201 S. College St., Charlotte, NC 28244. How to legally reduce your taxes by putting your family on the payroll.

Financial Independence: The Nissan Guide to Bootstrap Businesses, by the Editors of The Mother Earth News. 1984, Mother Earth News, Inc., 105 Stony Mountain Rd., Hendersonville, NC 28791. A very excellent book on how to start various bootstrap/moonlighting businesses. Published for Nissan Motor Corporation, so all the businesses involve the use of a small pick-up truck. One of the very best "Businesses You Can Start" books we have ever seen.

Homemade Money, by Barbara Brabec. 1984, Betterway Publications Inc., White Hall, VA 22987. Good book on starting a business in your home.

How To Start And Run A Successful Home Typing Business, by Peggy Glen. 1980, Aames-Allen Publishing Co., Main Street, Huntington Beach, CA 92648. Just what the title says.

Living Off The Country For Fun & Profit, by John L. Parker. 1978, Bookworm Publishing Co., PO Box 3037, Ontario, CA 91761. Different things you can do to earn money in the country.

Mail Order Moonlighting, by Cecil C. Hoge, Sr. 1976, Ten Speed Press, PO Box 7123, Berkeley, CA 94707. Excellent book on how to start a mail order business from your home, on the side.

Plants For Profit: A Complete Guide To Growing And Selling Greenhouse Crops, by Dr. Francis X. Jozwik. 1984, Andmar Press, Mills, WY 82644. How to start a greenhouse business, with emphasis on starting part-time.

Remnant Review, PO Box 8204, Ft. Worth, TX 76124. Conservative newsletter edited by Gary North. Often discusses the underground economy, and other issues of interest to readers of this book.

We Own It, by Peter J. Honigsberg, Bernard Kamoroff, and Jim Beatty. 1982, Bell Springs Publishing, PO Box 640, Laytonville, CA 95454. Good manual on how to start and run cooperatives, co-ops, and employee-owned ventures.

Why S.O.B.'s Succeed And Nice Guys Fail In A Small Business, by Anonymous. 1976, Morrison, Butterfield & Boyle Ltd., PO Box 15567, Phoenix, AZ 85060. Two-fisted manual on small business dirty tricks, and how to use them.

A Winning Thoroughbred Strategy, by Dick Mitchell. 1984, Cynthia Publishing, 4455 Los Feliz Blvd., Suite 1106, Los Angeles, CA 90027. How to use a microcomputer to make money at the races.

Women Working Home, by Marion Behr and Wendy Lazar. 1983, WWH Press, 24 Fishel Rd., Edison, NJ 08820. A fine book on starting a business in your home — not just for women, either.

Word Processing Profits At Home, by Peggy Glenn. 1984, Aames-Allen Publishing Co., Main St., Huntington Beach, CA 92648. How to start a home-based word processing business.

Working Free: Practical Alternatives To The 9 To 5 Job, by John Applegath. 1982, American Management Associations, 135 W. 50th St., New York, NY 10020. How to get out of the job economy and start your own business.

Working From Home, by Paul and Sarah Edwards. 1985, Jeremy P. Tarcher, Inc., Los Angeles. Excellent book on starting a business in your home.

FLEA MARKETS, CONVENTIONS, GARAGE AND YARD SALES

Auction!, by William C. Ketchum, Jr. 1980, Sterling Publishing Co., Inc., New York. All about auctions — how to buy and sell and save or make money.

Creative Cash, by Barbara Brabec. 1979, HP Books, PO Box 5367, Tucson, AZ 85703. How to moonlight by selling crafts, needlework, etc.

Flea Markets — Finding Products. AEA Business Research Report No. 360. 1981, American Entrepreneurs Association. How to locate products to sell at flea markets.

BARTER

Personal And Business Bartering, by James Stout. 1985, TAB Books Inc., Blue Ridge Summit, PA 17214. This book on barter covers aboveground barter, but is still very useful.

THE I.R.S., TAXES, AND FIDDLING THE BOOKS

ABC's Of Income Tax Avoidance, by Floyd Wright. 1985, Floyd Wright, PO Box 323, Grass Valley, Ca 95945. Aboveground tax protest book on avoiding banks, etc.

Audit-Block Guide: How To Lawfully Refuse An IRS Audit, by Marvin L. Cooley. 1982, Tax Facts Publishing Co., 525 E Baseline Rd., Mesa, AZ 85204. One of the most famous tax protestors tells how to keep the IRS out of your books.

Citizens Against Waste. 1511 K. St. NW, Washington, DC. Concerned citizens group, against waste in government.

Citizens For Just Taxation, PO Box 368, Dolton, IL 60419. An excellent source of books on the aboveground tax protest movement. If you want to fight the IRS in court, you can get a lot of ammunition here.

Confessions Of A Price Controller, by C. Jackson Grayson, Jr., with Louis Neeb. 1974, Dow Jones-Irwin, Inc. Homewood, IL 60430. The chairman of the Price Commission under Nixon describes the fiascoes that resulted when the government attempted to fix prices in the early 1970s.

Criminal Tax Fraud — Representing The Taxpayer Before Trial, by George Crowley and Richard Manning. 1976, Practicing Law Institute, 810 7th Av., New York, NY 10019. A manual for tax attorneys telling how to defend against charges of criminal tax fraud. Should be read by every Guerrilla Capitalist.

Forty Centuries Of Wage & Price Controls, by Robert Schuettinger and Eamonn Butler. 1978, The Heritage Foundation, Washington, DC. A history of over 4,000 years of attempts to control wages and prices, and why it never has worked.

The Great Income Tax Hoax, by Irwin Schiff. 1985, Freedom Books, PO Box 5303, Hamden, CT 06518. This fascinating book proves that there are no laws requiring anyone to file income tax returns, pay income taxes, or submit to IRS audits. By a prominent aboveground tax protestor.

How To Fight The I.R.S. —And Win! Volumes 1 & 2, by J. Eugene Wilson. 1977 and 1982, JC Printing Co., 3493 N. Main St., College Park, GA 30337. Excellent set of books on fighting back against the IRS in court, and how to block liens, etc.

How to Represent Yourself Before the IRS, by Bryan E. Gates. 1984, McGraw-Hill. An ex-IRS agent tells how to legally cope with the IRS.

How to Use the FOIA Effectively Against the IRS. 1982, Falcon Press, PO Box 60862, Sunnyvale, CA 94088. How to find out what the IRS has in their files on you.

I Want Out!, by Dennis Reome. Constitutional Protection Association, 7837 Greenback Ln. Suite #274, Citrus Heights, CA 85610. Booklet on IRS Form 4029, by filing which certain individuals (members of some religious groups) can claim conscientious exemption from Social Security and Self-Employment taxes. Some IRS employees claim this form doesn't exist!

Illegal Tax Protestors Threaten Tax System, Report by the Comptroller General of the United States. Reprinted by C.P.A., PO Box 645, N. Highlands, CA 95660. Government report on the "threat" posed by tax protestors.

Illegal Tax Protestor Training, IRS Manual. Reprinted by C.P.A., PO Box 645, N. Highlands, CA 95660. Reprint of IRS training manual on the dealing with tax protestors.

Inside IRS: How Internal Revenue Works (You Over), by Jeff A. Schnepper. 1979, Stein and Day, Briarcliff Manor,

NY. How the IRS works, including how the IRS processes an individual tax return, such as average deductions in each income bracket, and much other useful information.

The Internal Revenue Service: An Agency Out Of Control, by The National Coalition of IRS Whistleblowers. 1985, Freedom News Journal, 1301 N. Catalina St., Los Angeles, CA 90027. An excellent collection of horror stories about IRS Gestapo tactics.

Internal Revenue Service Practice and Procedure Deskbook, by Ira L. Ahafiroff. 1985, Practicing Law Institute, 810 7th Av., New York, NY 10019. A manual for tax attorneys on how to represent clients before the IRS.

Internal Revenue Service Strategic Plan. Document 6941 (5-84), Internal Revenue Service. This is the IRS blueprint for combatting tax evasion. Over 200 pages of stuff like "Programs To Better Address Compliance Problems Resulting From The Increasing Number Of Self-Employed Taxpayers." Published appropriately in 1984.

Investigative Methods For White Collar Crime, edited by William B. Moran. 1985, Loompanics Unlimited, PO Box 1197, Port Townsend, WA 98368. Edited government reports on how prosecutors issue search warrants, how they will try to "interview" your employees, etc.

IRS Special Agent's Handbook. Available from IRS, c/o Freedom of Information Rm., 111 Constitution Av. NW, Washington, DC 20224. Manual for IRS agents telling how to investigate tax evasion.

The Market For Liberty, by Morris and Linda Tannehill. 1970, Laissez Faire Books, 532 Broadway, 7th Fl., New York, NY 10012. Classic book showing how all government functions could be done better by private enterprise.

National Coaliton of IRS Whistleblowers. PO Box 7750, New York, NY 10116. Here is an organization that deserves your support! Headed by Paul DesFosses, ex-IRS agent, these guys expose the abuse of rights and Gestapo tactics of the IRS on a regular basis.

Power & Market: Government & The Economy, by Murray Rothbard. 1970, Sheed Andrews and McMeel Inc. Kansas City. Book by a prominent libertarian economist proving that government intervention into the economy never works.

The Screwing Of The Average Man, by David Hapgood. 1974, Bantam Books. An excellent book on how "The System" is rigged to screw *you.* In addition to taxes, the author covers banks, doctors, insurance companies, lawyers, and much more. One of the best books of its kind.

Spectrum: A Guide to the Independent Press and Informative Organizations, by Jim Corbett. 1985, Jim Corbett, 762 Avenue "N", SE, Winter Haven, FL 33880. A listing of mostly right-wing political organizations, with a good section on tax protest organizations and periodicals.

A Taxpayer Survey Of The Grace Commission Report, by William R. Kennedy, Jr. and Robert W. Lee. 1984, Green Hill Publishers, 722 Columbus St., Ottawa, IL 61350. A condensation of a government report on how the U.S. government wastes hundreds of billions of dollars.

Tax Wars, by Bill Kaysing. 1978, Eden Press, Fountain Valley, CA. Book on the different approaches the aboveground tax protest movement is using.

V.O.G.U.E. (Victims of Government United Everywhere), PO Box 3776, Washington, DC 20007. Anti-IRS group which has taken out some hard-hitting TV ads showing

Gestapo tactics of IRS. Some TV stations have refused to run these ads on the grounds that they "would undermine confidence in government!"

Win Your Personal Tax Revolt, by Bill Greene. 1981, Harbor Publishing Co., San Francisco. Various schemes and techniques for avoiding taxes, legal and quasi-legal.

Who's Afraid Of The IRS?, by Miss Lynn Johnston. 1983, Libertarian Review Foundation, 532 Broadway, New York, NY 10012. How-to-do-it book by an aboveground tax protestor. She hasn't paid taxes or filed returns for years, and tells how she gets away with it.

You CAN Beat City Hall, by W. Bernard Richland. 1980, Rawson, Wade Publishers, Inc., New York. Book on suing your city, town, county, or village.

"UNDERGROUND" INVESTING

Camouflage, US Army Field Manual FM 5-20. Reprinted by Desert Publications, PO Box 397, Cornville, AZ 86325. How to conceal various large objects from aerial and ground surveillance. Concentrates on military applications, but easily adaptable to civilian needs.

Checklist For Survival, by Tony & Jo-Anne Lesce. 1980, Paladin Press, PO Box 1307, Boulder, CO 80306. A good book on stockpiling essential items, forming support groups, etc.

The Construction Of Secret Hiding Places, by Charles Robinson. 1981, Desert Publications, PO Box 397, Cornville, AZ 86325. How to build secret hiding places in your home.

Eating Cheap, by Ragnar Benson. 1982, Paladin Press, PO Box 1307, Boulder, CO 80306. Making the most of what you have in the food department — how to save money on everything you eat.

Everyman's Guide To Tax Havens, by Adam Starchild. 1980, Paladin Press, PO Box 1307, Boulder, CO 80306. Good introduction to tax havens, and what they can do for you.

How To Profit From Offshore Banking, by A.V. Laurins and J.K. Rose. 1979, The Gold Depository and Loan Company, Inc., San Francisco. How to reduce taxes using offshore banks, and even how to start your own bank.

How To Survive Without A Salary, by Charles Long. 1981, Sterling Publishing Co. Inc., New York. How to get along on less money *and* how to make the most of what you have. Advocates the "Conservor Lifestyle." Excellent.

International Investing, by Douglas R. Casey. 1979, Everest House Publishers, New York. Excellent book on diversifying your investments by going overseas. Covers conditions in many likely foreign countries.

Secrets Of Offshore Tax Havens, by Robert Chappell. 1985, ABM Publishing Co., PO Box 1243, Wheatridge, CO 80033. How to avoid taxes by using offshore tax havens.

Simple Living Investments, by Michael Phillips. 1984, Clear Glass Publishing, Box 257, Bodega, CA 94922. Advocates investing in *yourself,* instead of *things.* The best investments are health, friends, skills, an austerity test, and for salaried people a rental house to be sold at age 55.

Tax Havens In the Caribbean, U.S. Justice Department. Reprinted by Paladin Press, PO Box 1307, Boulder, CO

80306. All about the "threat" of tax havens in the Caribbean, right from the mouth of the US government.

Tax Havens Of The World, by Walter H. and Dorothy B. Diamond. 1985, Matthew Bender & Co. Inc., 1275 Broadway, Albany, NY 12201. Considered the "Bible" of tax havens. Covers 50 tax-saving areas from Barbados to Liberia, from Andorra to Vanuatu.

Using An Offshore Bank For Profit, Privacy And Tax Protection, by Jerome Schneider. 1982, WFI Publishing Corporation, 2049 Century Park East, Los Angeles, CA. Good book on tax avoidance using offshore banks, including how to own your own offshore bank.

PRIVACY AND DODGING BIG BROTHER

Budd's Official Remailing Guide, by Wayne Budd. 1984, Wayne Budd Inc., RR No. 1, PO Box 63, Eldorado, Ontario, Canada K0K 1Y0. Book on how to use mail drops for privacy.

CIA Flaps And Seals Manual, Edited by John M. Harrison. 1975, Paladin Press, PO Box 1307, Boulder, CO 80306. How the government opens peoples' mail.

The Complete Guide To Financial Privacy, by Mark Skousen. 1983, Simon and Schuster, New York. Decent book on privacy, with emphasis on financial privacy.

Disguise Techniques, by Edmond A. MacInaugh. 1984, Paladin Press, PO Box 1307, Boulder, CO 80306. If you need to look different, this book tells you how.

Low Profile: How to Avoid the Privacy Invaders, by William Petrocelli. 1981, McGraw-Hill. How your privacy is invaded by both government and corporate snoopers, and how to avoid them.

Mail Order I.D., by Michael Hoy. 1985, Loompanics Unlimited, PO Box 1197, Port Townsend, WA 98368. Illustrated book on all the phony I.D. documents and cards you can buy through the mail. Everything from "Drivers Licenses" to "Ministerial" credentials!

The Outlaw's Bible, by E.X. Boozhie. 1985, Circle-A Publishers, 8608 E Hubbell, Scottsdale, AZ 85257. An excellent book on your Constitutional rights and how to use them. One of the finest books of its type ever written.

Paper Tripping Overseas, by Tony Newborn. 1985, Paladin Press, PO Box 1307, Boulder, CO 80306. How to get alternate I.D. in England, Australia, and New Zealand.

Personal And Business Privacy, by Bill Pryor. 1985, Eden Press, PO Box 8410, Fountain Valley, CA 92708. Spying and eavesdropping devices and methods, and how to avoid them.

The Postal Mail Cover, by P. Remington Adams. 1984, Alternative Technologies Information Service, 61 Gatchell St., Buffalo, NY 14212. Government snooping in the mail.

YOU WILL ALSO WANT TO READ:

☐ **13063** **SURVIVAL BARTERING,** *by Duncan Long.* People barter for different reasons — to avoid taxes, to obtain a better lifestyle — or just for fun! This book takes a look at the time coming where barter is no longer an interesting hobby, but a survival tool, a *necessity.* Learning *how* to barter now could be the best insurance you've ever had! *1986, 5½ x 8½, soft cover. $6.95.*

☐ **14046** **HOW TO BUY LAND CHEAP,** *by Edward Preston.* This classic book covers *all* the ways of buying land at rock-bottom prices. Where to start, what to do, buying land for back taxes, at auctions, buying tax land in Canada, inside tips, and much more. *1984, 5½ x 8½, 98 pp, illustrated, soft cover. $6.95.*

☐ **13027** **HOW TO LAUNDER MONEY,** *by John Gregg.* What every freedom lover should know! How to use corporations and business fronts to launder money, investing money without reporting it to the IRS, and much more! Clean up your act by laundering your money — professionally! *1982, 5½ x 8½, 64 pp, soft cover. $8.00.*

☐ **13044** **GUERRILLA CAPITALISM: How To Practice Free Enterprise in an Unfree Economy,** *by Adam Cash.* What good is "believing in" free enterprise if you don't *practice* it? This book shows you how to practice free enterprise in an unfree society — the ultimate book on financial privacy — it tells in step-by-step detail how to do business "off the books." *Sold for informational purposes only! 1984, 5½ x 8½, 172 pp, illustrated, soft cover. $10.95.*

And much more! We offer the very finest in controversial and unusual books — please turn to the catalog announcement on the next page.

Loompanics Unlimited, PO Box 1197, P. Townsend, WA 98368

Please send me the books I have checked above. I have enclosed $ _____ (including $3.00 for shipping and handling.

Name _____

Address _____

City/State/Zip _____

We use UPS delivery (unless otherwise requested) if you give us a street address.

CONTROVERSIAL AND UNUSUAL BOOKS!!!

Now available:
THE BEST BOOK CATALOG IN THE WORLD!!!

- *Large 8½ x 11 size!*
- *More than 500 of the most controversial and unusual books ever printed!!!*
- *YOU can order EVERY book listed!!!*
- *Periodic Supplements to keep you posted on the LATEST titles available!!!*

We offer hard-to-find books on the world's most unusual subjects. Here are a few of the topics covered IN DEPTH in our exciting new catalog:

- *Hiding/concealment of physical objects! A complete section of the best books ever written on hiding things!*
- *Fake ID/Alternate Identities! The most comprehensive selection of books on this little-known subject ever offered for sale! You have to see it to believe it!*
- *Investigative/Undercover methods and techniques! Professional secrets known only to a few, now revealed for YOU to use! Actual police manuals on shadowing and surveillance!*
- *And much, much more, including Locks and Locksmithing, Self Defense, Intelligence Increase, Life Extension, Money-Making Opportunities, and much, much more!*

Our book catalog is truly THE BEST BOOK CATALOG IN THE WORLD! Order yours today -- you will be very pleased, we know.

(Our catalog is free with the order of any book on the previous page -- or is $2.00 if ordered by itself.)

Loompanics Unlimited
PO Box 1197
Pt Townsend, WA 98368
USA